Representing
Yourself in Court
How to Win Your Case on Your Own

Devlin Farmer, Lawyer

Self-Counsel Press
(a division of)
International Self-Counsel Press Ltd.
Canada   USA

Self-Counsel Press acknowledges the financial support of the Government of Canada through the Canada Book Fund (CBF) for our publishing activities.

Printed in Canada.

First edition: 2015

Library and Archives Canada Cataloguing in Publication

Farmer, Devlin, author
    Representing yourself in court : how to win your case on your own/Devlin Farmer.

(Legal series)
Issued in print and electronic formats.
ISBN 978-1-77040-229-4 (pbk.).—ISBN 978-1-77040-994-1 (epub).—
ISBN 978-1-77040-995-8 (kindle)

    1. Trial practice—Canada.   2. Pro se representation—Canada.
I. Title. II. Series: Self-Counsel legal series

KE8422.F37 2015	347.71'0504	C2014-908257-6
KF8915.F37 2015		C2014-908258-4

MIX
Paper from
responsible sources
FSC
www.fsc.org FSC® C004071

Self-Counsel Press
(a division of)
International Self-Counsel Press Ltd.

Bellingham, WA   North Vancouver, BC
USA   Canada

Contents

Notice to Readers

Laws are constantly changing. Every effort is made to keep this publication as current as possible. However, the author, the publisher, and the vendor of this book make no representations or warranties regarding the outcome or the use to which the information in this book is put and are not assuming any liability for any claims, losses, or damages arising out of the use of this book. The reader should not rely on the author or the publisher of this book for any professional advice. Please be sure that you have the most recent edition.

This book and any download or associated electronic materials ("this book") provide general information about civil (not criminal) legal cases and offer information and techniques with respect to representing yourself in court proceedings generally. This book does not provide legal advice and nothing in it should be construed as such. Legal advice must come from a lawyer you consult, who can tell you why you should do something in your lawsuit or whether you should take certain actions. This book relates the author's personal historical experiences which may or may not be applicable to your particular case. Nothing in the book creates any rights, substantive or procedural, which are enforceable at law by any party.

Readers should research laws and deadlines specific to their jurisdictions. Readers are strongly urged to check primary sources where appropriate and use traditional legal research techniques to make sure information is correct.

Whenever possible, consult with a lawyer licensed in your jurisdiction about your particular case.

Thank You

Thanks to my early readers and all those who provided help along the way. A special thank you to three excellent lawyers who generously provided extra advice and insight: Thank you Mesdames Laura Atkinson, Kirsten McGhee, and Elizabeth Engerman. I am so grateful for your assistance.

Thanks also to AKF & SRF for the intermissions from writing, and to Tamsin for always giving and sharing so much.

An Introduction to Representing Yourself in Court

When you go to court you are asking a complete stranger (a judge) to make a decision about something he or she probably knows less about than you and the other party do.

Many of my clients have talked to me about wanting justice or wanting things to be fair. Who wouldn't want this? But going to court is not necessarily going to mean that what you think is fair and just is what the law and the trier of fact (the judge) in your case think is fair and just. The law is a blunt instrument for sorting out disputes. There are finer, more precise tools available, such as mediation. Try them first.

Going to court should be a last resort. Before going to court, you should have tried negotiating a solution to whatever it is you're dealing with; you should have also looked into alternatives to court such as mediation. Only when less adversarial options cannot offer a solution, is it time to seriously consider court. In other words, when there is no other way to solve a dispute, court is your last resort.

More and more self-represented people are appearing in court. (In some civil courts more than 50 percent of litigants are *pro se*.)

Lawyers' traditional bill-by-the-hour model and high retainer fees are simply out of reach for a large amount of average, working people.

The influx of non-lawyers into the Courts has necessitated change. Judges and court staff are gradually accepting that *pro se* litigants are here to stay. Self-help resources are increasingly available, and courts are more responsive to the needs of *pro se* litigants.

But changing the court system is not easy. Our courts rose out of exactly what their name suggests: a king's court. The language, rules, and procedure of going to court today hearken to a system that has roots in medieval England and which extend back to ancient Rome.

Today, you can still see barristers in black robes with ribbons around their necks bowing to a judge, hear lawyers throw around Latin phrases on a daily basis, and witness a formality and etiquette that has long since died out in other forms of society. Court is a hierarchal model with a judge sitting in an elevated position looking down on everyone else.

Appearing in court is intimidating. It can feel overwhelming. Here's a secret: Most lawyers are nervous going to court, and I'm no exception.

The antidote is preparation, or knowing what you're heading into and being ready for it. I like to break the process down into steps. When I'm at step one, I worry only about step one because I know that although step two is around the corner, I've prepared for what's in front of me at the moment. Preparation is not only the way to battle nervousness, it's also the key, the supreme weapon in fact, to winning your case.

The purpose of this book is twofold:

1. To give you an overview of the steps in the court process so that it does not feel as overwhelming when you represent yourself. It will help you to break the work you're going to need to do down into manageable steps with clear options. Because this book is an overview of going to court in Canada it is not specific to law in a particular province nor does it try to cite all the local rules on each topic. If I do quote any law, I will cite British Columbia law simply as an example. (Note that Federal and provincial law with the exception of Quebec is based on English common law. I am not licensed to practice law in Quebec and this book therefore does not cover how to go to provincial court in Quebec.)

You should always check what the specific law is in your jurisdiction and research how it applies to your unique case. As an overview, I hope this book will offer perspective as you do further research and choose your options. In other words, it is meant as a large scale map to help you see the big picture so that you can then zero in on what you need to know and do.

2. To give you a view into a lawyer's working office so that you can use some of the tricks of the trade that lawyers use. As in any profession, lawyers use certain tools and have certain methods to save time, to stay organized, and to smoothly advance a case. For example, most lawyers assemble a book for each trial called a Trial Book. They don't share these books with their clients; they are just a tool for the lawyer, and it's the lawyer's blueprint for a trial. I'll help you to make your own Trial Book so you can represent yourself and use this tool too.

This book is designed to address civil legal claims only. For example, the kind of litigants I had in mind while writing this book were family law litigants, small claims, and housing/eviction cases. (These are classes of litigants that are increasingly going to court or an administrative tribunal without a lawyer.) Sometimes I will talk about other kinds of civil law cases, but this book does not apply to criminal cases. As well, the focus of this book is for assistance with a judge-alone trial, not a jury trial. This is for several reasons: Including that jury trials are very difficult to run for self-represented persons. Jury trials may not be available for your kind of case (this will depend on your jurisdiction).

There are advantages to having a judge, who will likely be more experienced with self-represented persons and will have had training on deciding matters presented by self-represented persons, decide your case. (There may also be advantages to having a jury trial in your particular case and you would be well advised to seek the assistance of a lawyer in deciding whether to proceed with a jury or a judge-alone trial). My personal experience is with judge alone trials.

If you do have a jury trial, this book will still be helpful but you will need to do further research into the mechanics of a jury trial. I talk more about jury trials in Chapter 7: Pre-trial Procedures, Preparation, and Your Trial Book.

Because this book is an overview of the process of representing yourself in court, you will have to read up on the laws specific to your case. I will explain how to do that in Chapter 2: Learning the Law.

I also encourage you to read other books about how to present a case at trial. Different lawyers have different styles and different approaches. Many of us have concentrated on certain areas of law. For example, my background is mainly in family law, housing law, and professional ethics, though I've worked in a number of other areas too. Other lawyers may concentrate on, for example, personal injury.

Some books are written by university professors, not lawyers who appear in court. There is no comprehensive, ultimate guide, but take what you need from this and other resources so that you too will walk into court, nervous, yes, but prepared.

1. Vocabulary

Words are a big deal in law. Whole trials are about the interpretation of words. If there is a word in this book you don't understand, check the glossary in the download kit first. That will offer a basic definition. (If the word is important in your case, make sure you understand how that word is interpreted according to the law and case law in your jurisdiction.) If you still are unsure about a word in this book or in a legal resource, check a good law dictionary such as *Black's Law Dictionary* or *Canadian Law Dictionary* by Stephen Couglan et al.

2. Who's Who in the Court Process

You'll need to know who the people involved in the court process are:

- **Plaintiff:** The person who started the court case. Sometimes the plaintiff is called the claimant, complainant, applicant, or petitioner.

- **Defendant:** The person served with the court case. Sometimes the defendant is called the respondent.

- **Stenographer (also called a court clerk):** The person who records and transcribes the trial. This is done in case an error is made and an appeal is filed. It is usually possible for a party to listen to the recording of a hearing or to order a transcript of the hearing.

- **Interpreters:** Interpreters are often available if you (or someone else) are not comfortable proceeding in English.

- **Justice of the Peace:** Justices of the Peace are delegated certain powers to perform judicial duties. For example, a Justice of the Peace may hear a Small Claims Court matter in British

Columbia. A Justice of the Peace should be afforded the same courtesy and respect as a judge.

- **Registrars and registry staff:** When you go to a courthouse, there will be a registry where court papers are filed and kept for civil matters. Practically, this means there will be a location where you will have to stand in line to speak to registry staff.

  The staff who accept court papers for filing at these court registries are the gatekeepers for the court and if your papers are not in order, they may return them unfiled. Often, court staff can give you information about forms that you need to file. (Note that they cannot give you legal advice.)

  Tip: Treat registry staff, no matter how they treat you, with respect and courtesy. Sometimes registry staff can seem impolite. Trust me that keeping the registry staff on your side is a point in your favour. After all, they might share a lunchroom with your judge's clerk, or even your judge. Treat them well.

- **Sheriffs:** Peace officers are responsible for the protection of the courts in many provinces. They transport prisoners and can be seen standing in court to make sure order is maintained. If your cell phone rings, a sheriff will probably be the one telling you to turn it off.

- **Judge:** The judge is in charge of the court proceedings. A judge decides what evidence will be allowed, what motions may be heard, and how the case proceeds. At trial, if there is no jury, the judge applies the law to the facts he or she believes and makes the decision on the case.

  Judges are supposed to be impartial. This means, they should only decide the case on the evidence presented before them and not some preexisting bias they may have to one party or the other. Judges, like umpires or referees in sports games, make decisions on how the hearing or trial progresses. A judge might help you with the rules of court. However, a judge also might choose not to help you.

  One thing a judge can never do is give advice about your case. Only lawyers can provide legal advice. How willing a judge is to help you with Court Rules and procedure often depends on the judge you happen to get. Some are more willing than others to be helpful to a *pro se* litigant. In my experience, the trend is towards judges increasing in helpfulness to unrepresented persons.

Usually, you cannot choose your judge. Judges are usually assigned to your case based on the scheduling needs of the courthouse.

Judges belong to a particular court. For example, in British Columbia, there are judges who belong to the Superior Court, the Provincial Court, and the Court of Appeal. There are also federal judges who sit on the Federal Court.

Judges cannot:

- Deny your right to be heard. They can limit presentation of argument and evidence to what is material, relevant, and admissible. While judges will want to keep the process moving along, they have to give you a chance to try to prove your case.

- Talk to one side without the other being present unless there are exceptional circumstances at hand. This is called *ex parte* communication. It is considered unfair. When a case is, for example, very urgent, judges can hear from one party during an *ex parte* hearing. An *ex parte* hearing happens when one side does not give notice of a hearing to the other side either because the other side cannot be notified or because there is some emergency situation and notice would defeat the purpose of the relief sought (for example, if notice would cause the other side to destroy evidence), or it is impractical because of the urgent nature of the situation (for example, the other side is on the way to pick up the children and take them out of the jurisdiction). See detailed discussion of *Ex Parte* Hearings in Chapter 6: Motions and Temporary Orders.

- Refer you to a specific lawyer or recommend a specific lawyer to you.

- Give you legal advice.

- Violate the ethical rules judges are required to follow. For example, in British Columbia, Provincial Court judges are guided by the Ethical Principles for Judges and complaints about judges are looked into by the Chief Justice, who is responsible for supervising Provincial Court judges.

In a jury trial, the jury, not the judge, is the "trier of fact." The jury decides what evidence and witnesses to believe and makes the decision in the case.

3. The Court Process, a Big Picture Overview

Once you've tried alternatives to court such as mediation, negotiation, and arbitration, you will need to understand what you're getting into before you leap in. Learn the law in the area you will be going to court; the following sections give a big picture overview of the process, from start to finish. These topics will be covered in more detail in later chapters.

3.1 Step one: Filing in court

Once negotiations have broken down or perhaps because a limitation date is approaching, the first step for a plaintiff (the person starting a court case) is to file legal papers in court. Sometimes these papers are called, among other things, Statement of Claim, Petition, Complaint, or Notice of Claim. For convenience, I will simply refer to the papers that start a lawsuit as a Statement of Claim.

A Statement of Claim contains a description of the facts as you allege and what you want the Court to do (e.g., give you custody of your children, or perhaps pay you money in damages to compensate you for a loss).

If you are the person filing these papers you will be called either the plaintiff, the claimant, or a similar term. If you have been served with a plaintiff's claim, you are known as the respondent (because you are responding to the case), or defendant, or other term. Together, the plaintiff and the defendant are the "parties" to the court case.

If you disagree with the plaintiff's claims, your first step will be to file and serve on the other side your response, also known as an answer or defence (for ease of reference, I will call the document your "defence"). There are strict deadlines to do this. For example, if you were served with a notice of civil claim in British Columbia, your response must be filed and served within 21 days after service (Rule 3-3 BC Supreme Court Civil Rules).

When you file your response, it is also the time to make any claims you may have against the plaintiff. These are called "counterclaims," and the plaintiff will have an opportunity (and a deadline) to respond to any counterclaims.

3.2 Step two: Serve your Statement of Claim or Defence

Court rules will tell you what is required to deliver your Statement of Claim and other required papers (e.g., some jurisdictions also require a summons to come to court) to the person you are suing. This is known as "service." Typically, service to start a court case is required to be done by a third party who is not a party to and does not have any interest in the case. Frequently, service must be made by a process server such as a sheriff.

If you are a defendant, you will serve your defense on the other side after filing it at court.

3.3 Step three: Prepare, file, and serve any urgent or other pre-trial requests to the court

A request to the court is known as a "motion." If some aspect of the case is urgent, it is possible to go to court before a trial (trials often take a year or more from the start of the case, although some matters are quicker, for example, evictions). Typical urgent motions may be to ask the court to preserve property if there is a risk that it will be disposed of or if you need disclosure of documents or other evidence for your case. Another reason to make a motion early on is if you believe the other side has failed to make a valid legal claim; this is known as a motion to dismiss. Motions may be made shortly before the trial.

3.4 Step four: Trial preparation

Review and research the law, interview your witnesses, gather the evidence you are going to use at trial, and develop a theory of your case. Keep all information organized in files and begin to develop your Trial Book.

3.5 Step five: Discovery

Discovery is the process whereby you and the other side exchange the evidence that is relevant to the claims, counterclaims, and defenses in the case. It is a guiding principle of litigation that you and the other side have access to the evidence that either proves or disproves the important facts in a case.

For example, if you are suing someone you paid to paint your house but who failed to complete the job, some of your evidence shared in the discovery phase may include a receipt to show how much you paid and any contract you and the painter signed.

Discovery not only includes exchanging documents, it can include exchanging photographs, recordings, and anything else you will rely on at trial to prove your case or disprove the other side's case. The discovery process includes tools to gather information such as examinations for discovery (an opportunity to ask the other side or witnesses questions under oath).

3.6 Step six: Negotiation and mediation

As discovery uncovers evidence, as each side learns more about the strengths and weaknesses of their case, and as the parties' emotional feelings may cool or wear down, new opportunities for a settlement will present themselves. Negotiations may take place by letter or at in-person meetings. Using a trained mediator to facilitate discussions is a very helpful tool at this stage.

3.7 Step seven: Pre-trial conference

Often, court rules require the parties to attend a meeting or hearing with a judge before the trial. The purpose of this meeting is for the court to ascertain whether the parties are ready for trial. It can also be an opportunity to settle or resolve some or all matters in the case.

3.8 Step eight: Trial

Trials normally do not proceed until discovery is complete (the parties have shared all information required by court rules and are satisfied that discovery is complete) and the court is assured that you are ready for trial. Frequently, a trial will take place anywhere from six months to several years after a Statement of Claim was first filed. (Evictions are a notable exception. They may only take a couple of months from filing to trial.)

Trials may last from a couple of hours to a couple of weeks, depending on the complexity of the case, amount of evidence, and the number of witnesses.

3.9 Step nine: Appeals, enforcement of court orders, and modifications

If you've won your case, you still might need to go back to court to ask the court to make the other side pay what they've been ordered to pay. You may, for example, need a court's permission to garnishee a bank account.

If you've lost, you might be considering whether an appeal would be successful or not.

At some point in the future, an outstanding court order may no longer be appropriate and you may wish to change it. This is known as a modification application.

4. Administrative and Quasi-Judicial Proceedings

Sometimes the decision-making power for certain kinds of disputes does not lie with the provincial or federal court system. Instead, it will lie with an administrative tribunal. For example, in British Columbia housing cases such as evictions are decided by a Hearing Officer at the Residential Tenancy Board (RTB).

Administrative tribunals generally have their own rules which are similar to court proceedings insofar that the rules will tell you what steps to take in the legal dispute (procedure), and they are similar to court proceedings. However, administrative proceedings are often less formal than court and may have much shorter timelines. For example, you often will sit at a table with the Hearing Officer in an administrative tribunal rather than standing before a judge in a courtroom. Frequently, rules of evidence are relaxed.

This book will help you with administrative proceedings too. As with any legal dispute, you should first read the rules that apply to the administrative proceeding. You may then find sections of this book helpful when preparing for your hearing such as creating your own Trial Book.

5. Is It a Good Case?

Whether it is a good case is the hardest question for a *pro se* litigant to answer. You might be 100 percent certain that you are morally right but that doesn't mean a court will decide the case in your favour. See Chapter 2 for a discussion of applying the law to the facts of your case. The bottom line: Generally, you should not go to court unless the odds are at least 50 percent or higher of winning.

The way I like to think of it is like this: Ask yourself, is it likely that you will be better off having gone to trial than not? Ideally, to help you make that determination, get legal advice. You may be able to find lawyer referral services who offer a discounted fee for an initial consultation with a lawyer. Or there may be a service in your area where you can speak to a lawyer at the courthouse for free. If you can't get legal advice, do your research carefully and factor in the possibility that, in any case, you might lose. Are you ready for that risk?

5.1 Is there a legal issue?

A common reason for *pro se* cases to be thrown out of court by a judge is because the case fails to state a claim upon which relief may be granted. It is important to be clear about two things:

1. What your legal problem is.

2. What the law can do about it.

There are many problems which exist in the world that do not have legal solutions. Judges can only make orders where there is a legal reason to make the order. For example, the judge cannot order someone to believe that astronauts never landed on the moon. However, a judge can make a finding that someone broke a rule.

When you are asking the judge to do something about your legal problem you are asking for a remedy. For there to be a legal issue, there must be a remedy. This is also known as "relief." For example, in a dispute about money a court may order one party to pay the other party a certain sum of money. Payment of that money is the remedy (or relief) that one party was seeking. In a dispute about who certain property belongs to, the Court may order that the property be retained by one person. Keeping that property is the remedy. In a dispute about parenting time, a court may order which days of the week a child spends with a parent. How much time that party gets is the remedy.

Identifying whether there is in fact a legal issue can be tricky, but it is an essential first step. Let's look at some examples.

Legal Issue or Not?

John refuses to pay Sara for repairing his fence because he says Sara did a bad job.

Yes, it's a legal issue because the court can determine if there was a contract between John and Sara and whether its terms were fulfilled. The court can decide if John should pay Sara or not.

Seth's grocery store has stopped stocking his favourite candies. Seth decides to sue to force the store to restock his candies, or pay him damages.

No, there really isn't a legal issue here. Seth and the grocery store didn't have a contract that the store supply him with his candies. In this situation, there is no reason for a court to tell a grocery store what to stock.

Ann's neighbour never says hello to her when she greets him.

No, this isn't a legal issue. A Court cannot make your neighbour be polite.

A neighbour and I are in a dispute about a fence that I built. I feel it is on my property. My neighbour claims that it is on his property. He puts flyers on all the cars in my neighbourhood stating that I am a trespasser and a criminal. He tells me that he will tear down the fence.

Yes, there are legal issues here. The first is whether I had a right to build the fence and, if not, whether my neighbour has grounds to tear it down. The second is whether the neighbour defamed me (libelled me) by putting flyers on cars stating that I was a trespasser and a criminal.

6. The Cost of Litigation

Going to court, even without a lawyer, can be expensive. You should be aware of the following potential costs before starting, or defending, a lawsuit:

1. **Filing Fees:** Different courts have different fees for starting a court action. When you start a court action, you will have to file in the court registry a notice that sets out your claims. Typically, there is a fee to file these papers. (If you have low income, you may be able to apply to the court to cancel these fees.) For example, in British Columbia the fee to file a case seeking damages of less than $3,000 in Small Claims Court is currently $100. Also, if you need to file other papers in court before your trial, such as a motion for temporary orders or a pre-trial brief, there may be a fee to file these papers.

    If you win your case, the judge may order the other side to pay these fees (see Costs, below). However, most cases settle before trial and these fees are not recovered.

2. **Service Fees:** Usually to start a court case you have to serve a filed copy of your complaint on the other side. Court rules may require you to pay a process server, constable, or sheriff to hand the papers to the other side. If the person to be served is cooperative, these fees are typically less than $100 but if the person being served is uncooperative, is difficult to find, or lives out of province, these fees can climb.

3. **Examination for Discovery:** If you choose to examine the other side or a witness in a sworn examination, you will have to pay to rent a place to do so and for a stenographer (a typist) to record and then type the examination. You will also have to pay for copies of the transcripts including a copy for the court. You may also have to pay the witness a small fee for being available and, if he or she lives outside of the jurisdiction, you may have to pay for travel costs.

4. **Other costs:** Photocopying (e.g., at trial you need at least three copies of most documents — one for yourself, one for the judge, and one for the other side), long-distance charges, fax charges, and postage are all likely if you are going to mount a trial. (Law firms call these expenses "disbursements" and they are typically added to your bill.)

5. **Court costs:** A court can order that one party pay the legal expenses of the other party. This can happen if you lose at trial. So, even if you don't hire a lawyer, it is possible that you will have to pay for a portion or all of the other side's lawyer if you lose.

6. **Stress:** Legal disputes are very stressful. There is often an emotional layer that undergirds the dispute. (Often, in the midst of a legal battle, it is very difficult to ascertain what we really want and need from feelings of what we deserve and who is right and wrong. Being emotionally supported — for example, through a counsellor and a network of family and friends — will help you in your legal battle.)

   The Court system is an adversarial system. It is built on the premise that the winning side will be able to withstand legal tests and challenges to their case. If your case is built on your testimony, that legal testing will be aimed at you and you will have to endure vigourous cross-examination. The stress of going to trial may affect your health as well as your pocketbook. You will need to decide whether the increased stress and its impact on your loved ones is worth it.

7. **Time:** You may have to invest considerable time in preparing for a trial. I know that whenever I am, or a lawyer I know is, preparing for trial, everything else has to take a backseat. In the weeks before a trial, I always end up working evenings and weekends. You may have to take time off work to prepare, which will cost you too.

   Court typically involves lots of court forms; if you are someone who hates doing, for example, your own taxes, you may find the forms at court and the amount of time you'll have to invest in filling them out daunting. That being said, don't hesitate to seek assistance with forms from court staff, free lawyer services or, even better, hire a lawyer to fill out the forms or do some things but not all (we'll cover this later).

7. So, Is It Time to Go to Court?

Knowing when to go to court is very difficult to figure out. Taking that step of filing in court and serving the other side with court papers is not a step you can take back. It is almost always interpreted as aggressive and as an escalation of a dispute. Resolving your dispute at the kitchen table or over a cup of coffee becomes unlikely after you file in court. That doesn't mean that the case won't settle — most cases do settle — it just means the tenor of communications and negotiations with the person you are in conflict with will probably change. So, what are the factors that suggest it is time to go to court? (These factors are built on the assumption that you have a good case, meaning that the odds are you will come out in a better position than when you went in.)

7.1 Factors indicating it is time to go to court

Following are some factors that indicate it may be time to go to court:

1. **Negotiations are stalled:** You've tried to talk to the other side, but they are unwilling to negotiate. Or their last offer was, they told you, "final," and it is far from acceptable to you. You need to jump-start things, get the other side's attention, let them know you are serious; filing in court may be the way to do this.

2. **There is an emergency:** The other side is about to do something that will affect the outcome of the case. If you are arguing about a sum of money that is in his or her possession, and he or she is about to take an expensive cruise and spend all that money, it may be time to file in court and ask a judge to order that the money not be spent until after a trial. Or, if you are arguing about where you child lives, and you find out the other side has purchased plane tickets to move themselves and the child across the country, it is likely time to file in court.

3. **A limitation deadline is approaching:** Most kinds of claims are time-limited. That means that they have to be filed before a specific time period expires. These deadlines range from days to years. Understanding limitation deadlines can be complicated but it is extremely important not to miss a limitation deadline. Missing a deadline can mean the end of your lawsuit or that the other side's lawsuit is successful. If you have not filed in court, and even if you are still talking to the other side and settlement looks possible, you should file in court if

not doing so will mean that you miss a limitation deadline. The other side might be negotiating just to stall you filing so that you cannot bring your case to court. Note that in some jurisdictions, using Alternative Dispute Resolution (ADR) processes may suspend or put a hold on the deadline clock.

4. **Things are getting worse:** The dispute is escalating. Whatever went wrong continues to go wrong and it is getting worse. Things need to change and talking isn't helping.

5. **The playing field is not even:** The other side is bullying you. You don't feel you can stand up to them. They have a lawyer who is running circles around you and you don't understand what he or she is saying. If you don't feel that you can get a fair deal with the other side without help, court might be an option. You may also want to consider mediation, where a trained mediator will be able to use certain tools to level the playing field. Also, a trained mediator should tell you if mediation cannot help to level the playing field and thus when court is appropriate.

7.2 Factors indicating it is not time to go to court

Following are some factors that indicate it is not time to go to court:

1. The other side is showing signs of changing their position: Maybe their previous "final offer" turns out not to be so final and they've made you a new settlement offer.

2. You keep putting off the dispute: The court process involves a strict schedule of deadlines. You will have to keep these marked in a calendar. Missing a deadline can have severe consequences, including dismissal of your case if there isn't a good reason for the missed deadline. If you aren't committed to following the strict calendar of a court proceeding, maybe you shouldn't go to court.

3. It will cost you more money to go to court than you could win even in the best case scenario.

4. You would rather just walk away from the dispute.

5. You have obtained a legal opinion and a second legal opinion, both of which recommend against going to court. Or your legal research makes it clear that you will likely lose your case.

6. The other side has no ability to pay you the money you feel they owe you or to do what you want them to do. So, even if a court makes a decision in your favour, you will not get what you want.

8. Be Informed

Some people have the choice of choosing to walk away from a legal dispute. Others are locked into it. In either case, educate yourself and make an informed decision.

Moving forward means preparation: Read this whole book before you begin and use it (and other similar books that you find helpful) in tandem with resources from your jurisdiction that explain court procedure and the law. There are wonderful resources now available to help *pro se* litigants. Statutes, cases, do-it-yourself forms, and explanations of the law are available online and in court libraries.

Be careful when doing an Internet search, however, that you are using sites that are for your province and your kind of legal issue. The sites I recommend and are most trusted are sites created by the courts themselves, and sites created by legal aid organizations and law libraries. For further discussion of learning about the law and court procedure see Chapter 2: Learning the Law.

Some critical information before you decide which way to go:

1. Be aware of any limitation periods. If you are close to a limitation period, you should seriously consider filing in court.

2. Find a way to talk to a lawyer about your case. See Chapter 4: Lawyers.

3. Don't panic. The fact that you are reading this means you're ahead of most people. You're on your way to being prepared.

4. As you move forward, you will have to think about the cost versus the benefit of court. Most cases settle. Part of the process of preparing for court is simply to gather the information you need to evaluate what a settlement you can live with looks like.

Part One
Before the Trial

1

Settlement and Alternatives to Court

Most legal disputes end up settling. Courts generally expect that you and the other side will be trying to come up with a solution that both can live with so that a trial can be avoided. Sometimes settlement happens before the case is filed in court. This is often ideal as it saves the parties the cost of filing as well as avoiding creating any public record. Sometimes cases settle after pre-trial hearings. Other times, cases settle in the court hallway moments before the trial begins.

1. What Is Settlement?

Black's Law Dictionary defines a settlement, also known as a settlement agreement, as "[a]n agreement ending a dispute or lawsuit." However, settlement may also end part of the dispute. For example, in a divorce you may settle all the terms relating to property but still pursue a trial with respect to parenting time.

A settlement can be the following:

- Oral (e.g., you reach a deal on the phone).

- Oral but confirmed in writing (you exchange letters or emails confirming you've reached a settlement).

- Written in settlement agreement, which is essentially a contract.

- Oral but confirmed and approved by a judge in a court order.

- Written but confirmed and approved by a judge in a court order.

Ideally, settlement is in a written settlement agreement signed by both parties, or turned into a court order consented to by both parties. Your jurisdiction may have specific requirements for a settlement agreement.

1.1 Is settlement win-win?

Well, actually, it's more like Not Lose-Not Lose. Both parties will have to make compromises but there are huge benefits to avoiding a trial.

Here are some advantages of reaching a deal without a trial:

- **Control:** You are in control of the outcome. One of the risks of allowing a judge to make a decision is that you might lose. Or that the relief you get if you win really is not enough to have been worth the expense and stress of a trial. Reaching a settlement allows you to manage your risk so that you do not lose everything and have control over designing a solution to the dispute.

- **Privacy:** Most trials are public. A term of the agreement might be to keep the settlement terms confidential. (This may not be possible for all cases.)

- **Cost:** Though you are self represented, going to court still carries fees and expenses as well as the risk that the court might award costs against you if you lose.

- **Continued relationship with the other side:** Settlement usually results in a lower degree of anger and animosity between you and the other side. If you need to have a professional business relationship with the other person, or want him or her to not speak ill of you in the community or, most importantly, if you are engaged in a family law dispute and need to have a continued relationship for the sake of children, a negotiated settlement will help to ease the transition to a more business-like, less hostile post-dispute relationship.

- **Enforcement:** An agreement is more likely to lead to both parties fulfilling what the agreement requires them to do (e.g., pay a certain sum of money) than when a court imposes a requirement. Especially in family law proceedings, the cooperation that agreements require can benefit future interactions and have less negative impact on third parties or children.

- **Less stress than a trial:** Without the strict court rules and preparation for a trial, as well as the formality of court, any form of settlement is bound to be less stressful than a trial. That being said, preparation is still key to reaching a settlement and there will be some stress.

1.2 What are the disadvantages of a settlement?

A settlement should be voluntary. If you are feeling forced into settling, take a breath, get a second opinion (preferably from a lawyer), and remind yourself that a trial is always an option. You should not agree to a settlement if you are feeling forced into it.

Some of the disadvantages of settlement may be:

- **Enforceability:** You may be worried that a written agreement doesn't carry as much weight as a court order. Depending on your jurisdiction, it may require a few more steps to enforce an out-of-court settlement versus a court order. However, written agreements that are legally valid with enforceable terms usually can be enforced through the court system.

- **Nobody "wins":** Sometimes people feel so strongly about their position that they do not want to compromise. If you are feeling this way, a trial might be the only solution for you.

- **It might not work:** Settlement negotiations or mediation might not actually lead to settlement. You may spend time and money on a process that does not actually get you the settlement you wanted. However, often going through this process can help you learn about the other side's position which may be helpful at trial.

2. How to Get to Settlement: It Takes Two

There are different styles and tools you can use to settle a case. The only really essential ingredient is that both parties must voluntarily participate in the process. You cannot settle a case with only one person. If the other side is unwilling to engage in any of the options described below, you should consider going to court.

2.1 When Is a Deal a Deal? Offer and Acceptance

Though this book is not intended to provide you with an explanation of what the law is (it's your job to go out there and do the research for your jurisdiction and area of law), it is important to be aware of a basic principle underlying negotiations that comes from contract law: offer and acceptance. When you make an offer and it is accepted, a contract is created.

A contract is enforceable. That means, if you breach a term of the contract (don't do something the contract says you will do), the other side can go to court to ask for damages for your breach. Thus, whenever you make an offer be very careful about what you are offering because those terms could become the terms of a contract between you and the other side. This applies to oral offers and oral acceptances as much as written. It is just harder to prove what the terms of an oral contract are if the two of you don't have the same account of what those terms are.

2.2 Take notes

Always take notes of telephone or in-person negotiations. And write out what your offer is ahead of time so that you remember to offer all the terms. For example, let's say you are in a dispute with a painter. You paid a deposit, the painter used a colour that wasn't what you agreed on, and the job is sloppy. Now, you feel you will have to hire a new painter. You offer the painter a deal: He repaints the room and you will pay him the full contract price. The painter agrees. However, let's say that you meant the offer to be conditional on the work being done within the next week. You can't add that term in later without the painter's consent. (You should try to get his consent but the painter could say that a deal had been struck and refuse to add a new term.)

3. Types of Alternative Dispute Resolution

3.1 Verbal negotiations

Negotiation usually takes place right from the moment that the dispute occurs right up to the minutes before the judge makes a decision. (Yes, you can even negotiate a settlement during a trial.) Negotiation can be informal (a phone call) or formal (a settlement conference meeting). When you negotiate you should be thoughtful and careful. In other words, you should be strategic.

3.1a Negotiating by phone

Whether it is a lawyer or the other party on the line, phone calls, for me, somehow tend to never quite work as well as face-to-face negotiations. However, they are worth a try. Usually a phone call is good for settling a particular part of a case. For example, if you need to work out when you will share information about the case (see Discovery, Chapter 5).

If you reach agreement by phone, it is always a good idea to follow up with a letter confirming the terms of the deal. For example, if you and the other side agree to exchange a list of witnesses in two weeks you'd simply write, "This is to confirm our conversations of [date]. We agreed to each provide to the other party a list of potential witnesses and their contact information for trial. We agreed to exchange these lists no later than two weeks from the date of our phone conversation. I look forward to your list. Thank you." If you reach a deal on a major issue (e.g., how much money the other side will pay you for you to not go to court), you should also put that deal in a settlement agreement (a written agreement signed by both sides).

3.1b In-person settlement meeting

An in-person meeting is a great opportunity to settle a case. If the other side brings a lawyer, remember that that lawyer is working for the other side and will not provide you with legal advice. If you reach agreement in person, you can confirm the terms of your settlement by writing an agreement together. Sometimes you will just sketch out the terms as points. This is sometimes known as a Memo of Understanding which you will later redraft together as an agreement.

If the other side is represented, they may suggest the meeting. They may call it a "three-way" meeting. (If you had a lawyer, it would be called a "four-way meeting.") It may feel intimidating going to a lawyer's office, and kind of like two against one. You may want to ask a friend to come to the meeting (with the other side's consent) for moral support. (Having another person present may affect the confidentiality of the meeting because that third party could talk about what happened at the meeting or even be subpoenaed into court about it. There may be ways around this, however, and the benefit of you feeling supported may outweigh the risk of information being disclosed.)

You could suggest that the meeting happen on more neutral turf, such as at your local courthouse or library (check ahead to see if such a space is available).

If things feel uncomfortable during a settlement meeting, suggest that everyone take a break. If the meeting is unproductive or you feel you are being coerced, politely but firmly tell the other side that you are ending the meeting. Always remember that settlement negotiations are voluntary and you can end them at any time.

Negotiating Techniques

I sometimes think of lawyering as being a professional negotiator. Here are some techniques that you may find useful (I use all of them):

- Write out and practice what you are going to say beforehand.

- Don't offer your bottom line right away. Go into each negotiation with a bottom line, and stick to it, but don't offer it right out of the gate.

- Be reasonable. Make an offer you know the other side might accept. Keep things in the zone of reasonable, possible, and fair for both of you. (Some negotiators don't like to do this right away. They hope that putting the bar unreasonably high will mean that when they move into the reasonable zone, their more reasonable offer will look better. In my experience being unreasonable comes back to bite you.)

- Think about what the other side wants. Figure out a way to give them what they want but also in a way that doesn't take away too much from what you want. Be sure to make any offer attractive to them by adding whatever "sweeteners" you can. For example, in a contract dispute about lumber which you bought, but which you want to return to the supplier because you feel it isn't what you ordered, you may know the supplier really doesn't want to spend the time and money to have a truck pick up the product. You have a truck and can deliver it. When you make your monetary offer, also offer to deliver the product. A small sweetener can tip an offer that the other side is hedging on to acceptance.

- Always be polite. Never resort to insults or cheap shots. You may think the other side is a lying, good for nothing cheat. Telling them that is not going to help you get what you want from them. (Never ever put anything insulting in an email or letter. Chances are it'll come up at trial and make you look bad.) Instead, show them by a carefully reasoned explanation that they risk losing more money in court than if they settle with you, today, right now. If the negotiation is in person, suggest at the beginning some ground rules. For example, everyone will be polite and no interrupting each other.

- Know when to pull the plug on rudeness. If the other side resorts to name calling or attacking you personally, or if the conversation is no longer about negotiating a deal but about what a crappy person you are, you should first allow that some steam may need to be let off. You might need to grin and bear a little, but don't take the bait and get into it. If it continues, you probably need to end the negotiation. I recommend simply telling the other side that you don't feel the current tone is productive and that you're going to either hang up or leave, and doing just that.

- Don't act desperate. If the other side is not returning your calls or shoots down every settlement offer you make, don't panic. There is a process that a legal dispute follows and if negotiations aren't working, then simply move on to the next step. Try proposing a formal meeting or sending them a settlement letter or demand letter. Use another tool. Be patient and reasonable; trust that in time, the dispute will be over because if settlement doesn't work, there is always a trial at the end of the road.

3.2 The art of written negotiations: Letters and emails

Putting your words in writing can be very powerful. Not only can a well-written, businesslike letter be more persuasive than a conversation, it can focus the parties on the actual issues at hand and take away some of the personal attacks. Perhaps most important, it creates a record and that record may eventually have legal significance.

3.2a Letters

Generally, settlement letters are not admissible in evidence at trial. The thinking behind this is to allow you and the other side to have a frank and open communication about the dispute that will not be held against you. However, settlement letters may come into evidence in certain limited circumstances:

- The letter is not a settlement letter. You don't actually make an offer and in some way the letter proves or disproves a material fact in dispute.

- After the trial, regarding costs.

- As proof a settlement was reached or evidence of the terms of the settlement.

With respect to costs, in many jurisdictions what a formal settlement letter can do is award costs to the successful party at trial if they win more at trial than they offered in their settlement letter. For example, let's imagine that you wrote to the other side and offered a settlement of $10,000 and they refused that offer. If after trial you were awarded $12,000, you may be eligible for costs. The reason this is done is as an incentive to settle. In other words, a formal settlement letter is a reminder that if you do not accept a reasonable settlement offer, you will have to pay extra if you waste the Court's time by taking the matter to trial. A formal settlement letter is a very useful tool in leveraging settlement.

There may be certain elements necessary for a formal settlement letter in your jurisdiction.

If you receive a settlement letter from the other side, here are some options:

1. If you agree with everything and do not want any added or different terms, write back and say that you accept the terms of their proposal. Mention their letter specifically by date so that it is clear what you are agreeing to.

2. If you agree with some things but not others, you can write back to explain what you accept and what you do not. Propose any new terms you wish. This will likely be considered a counterproposal which the other side can either accept or reject. Consequently, the initial offer is considered rejected and cannot be later accepted by you.

3. If you disagree with everything, you have several choices:

   • Do nothing. I do not recommend this. Otherwise the other side might argue that you have accepted the offer.

   • Write back and say that you cannot accept the offer. You do not have to provide reasons unless you think those reasons may help the other side to change their position.

   • Write back, say that you do not accept the offer and make a counterproposal. This is what I typically do.

One final word about letters. As a *pro se* litigant who is up against a represented party, you may be on the receiving end of letters that claim to be settlement letters. But in fact, most of the letter is a blistering personal attack delivered in a tone that sets your blood boiling. Letters from a certain old-school caste of lawyers frequently adopt all the bitter dregs of your dispute and hurl them back at you all under the letterhead of an esteemed law firm. Instead of the basic facts, these letters seize on all the trigger issues. They are especially common in family law litigation. (Fortunately, they are becoming less common.) Sadly the last thing these letters do, in my opinion, is promote settlement. Why are they written? See the "cc" at bottom of the letter under the lawyer's (arrogantly large) signature? That means "carbon copy." It will probably say "client" after "cc." That means a copy of the letter has been sent to the other party. The letter may have been written as a demonstration of zeal and advocacy by the lawyer for his or her client. What the client doesn't realize is that in this battle, probably no one will ever see that letter. Not realizing this, recipients of these kind of letters often think they need to respond in kind. Refute every allegation and make a few of your own. In fact, you don't need to get into it. The best response is to focus on whether the offer in the letter is good or bad and respond to that. For example, state that you have a different point of view with respect to the facts as alleged in the letter and move on to responding to the offer. When you get one of these letters, you can console yourself with one thing. The letter probably cost the other side at least an hour in legal fees (that is several hundred dollars).

3.2b Emails

The risk with email is that you might click "send" before you're ready and the other side may quickly accept an offer that you haven't fully thought out. That's why I recommend that any written communication that offers settlement be written as a proper formal letter. Yes, you can attach that letter to an email later. But write it in Word so that you don't press send too soon. I like to write a settlement letter, but not send it right away; instead, I give it a day before I look at it again. That way, I approach it fresh and find little mistakes or omissions, or realize that perhaps I could tighten up some wording. If possible, have a legal advocate look it over. Once the letter has aged at least a day this way, then send it.

However, I understand that the other side might write you a settlement offer by email and that might lead to some back and forth emailing; offer followed by counteroffer and so on. If you do end up making a deal via email, I still recommend that you confirm the content of that settlement by letter or sign an agreement with the other side. If you don't do this and later want to make the other side follow through on what they agreed to, you could have difficulty. This is because a chain of emails can be confusing.

3.2c Demand letters and settlement offers

A demand letter is not very different from a settlement offer. Generally, demand letters are one of the first steps after informal negotiation has broken down. The letter will set out the facts of the dispute, quote applicable law (this is not always necessary) and demand what is wanted to end the dispute. Often it will contain a deadline for response. If a deadline is not included in any settlement offer the offer remains open for acceptance until the person who made the offer says he or she is withdrawing or rescinding the offer, or the person to whom the offer is made rejects the offer. A counterproposal is generally considered a rejection of an offer.

When you include the facts tell your story in simple, basic terms. Don't give away too much information at this point but provide enough that if a stranger were to read the letter, he or she would understand it (although a stranger shouldn't read it; settlement letters are not supposed to be disclosed). The facts should identify the injury or loss that you suffered. If there is a lawyer on the other side, this is the stranger you want to convince. If there isn't, then you should imagine that a judge might one day be looking at the letter for purposes of awarding costs to you. You want the judge to understand your point of view.

Include the law in simple terms. Don't go overboard with citing cases etc., unless your case really does turn on a different interpretation of the law. Just keep it simple. Here is your opportunity to say why you should have the relief you are asking for.

Spell out the terms of your offer very clearly. In fact, the only essential element of a demand letter is the terms for settlement. (After all, you and the other side disagree on the facts and the law anyway.) If there is more than one term, it is helpful to set them out in numbered paragraphs. If the terms are ambiguous (in other words, if there could be more than one interpretation of them), then the settlement might not actually be enforceable by a court. The terms should specify who, what, where, and when. For example, if your offer is to accept a payment of $2,000 as settlement, you might write: "Mr. Jones will pay the sum of $2,000 by money order or certified cheque to me on or before March 1, 20XX." If you don't specify this level of detail, you might find yourself negotiating the details later and potentially having the deal fall apart.

As I've mentioned earlier regarding emails, it's good idea to let the letter sit for a day so that you can be sure the offer is what you want to do and also to catch any errors you may have made. Then, once you've made any corrections and, if possible, had a lawyer review it, you're ready to date and sign it.

Photocopy the letter with your signature on it and keep a copy for your records (and to show the court if needed for purposes of post-trial costs if available). If you are concerned that the other side might claim they never received the letter, send it so that there is some tracking number or signature required and keep post office receipts.

Generally, I do not email formal settlement letters that I might use in court. This is because email, in my opinion, does not make the same impression nor is it taken as seriously as good, old-fashioned paper, type, and a personal signature. Email also does not provide proof of receipt. A print out of an email you've sent only shows that you *sent* the email, not that it was received.

Should your letter have a deadline? Sometimes yes, sometimes no, but a deadline that says an offer expires may invalidate the ability to use the letter to collect costs, although a deadline can motivate the other side to take you seriously and to settle the case. For example, you can state that if you do not receive a response by a certain date that your offer is withdrawn. (You can also state that if you have not received a response by a certain date that you will do certain things, such as that you will have to file in court. Any statement like this should be scrupulously honest and you should intend to do the thing you are saying; also note that lawyers should not threaten to file or not file criminal charges.)

Write "Without Prejudice" at the top of the demand letter. This will let the other side know that the letter is a settlement offer and should not be used against you later.

Some jurisdictions have specific laws that apply to letters. Research what is needed for a demand letter to be effective in your jurisdiction.

4. Bill Eddy's BIFF Response

Bill Eddy is an attorney, mediator, and therapist in California, and the president of the High Conflict Institute which has wonderful resources for people caught in high-conflict disputes. One of his most famous and well-used techniques for written and especially email communications is to respond to hostile emails with a "BIFF Response": Brief, Informative, Friendly, and Firm. His rules for a BIFF Response can be applied to any communication: phone calls, letters, or in-person meetings, whether you start things or are responding. (For more information, go to www.biffresponse.com).

Brief means that you are letting the other side know that you don't want to get into a prolonged back and forth dispute. It also means there is less for the other side to criticize.

Informative means keeping the communication to the facts. Correct mistakes made by the other side by making the accurate statements you want to make.

Friendly is important because a friendly communication is more likely to be given consideration (as opposed to reaction) than an unfriendly one, and thus will help to end your dispute.

Firm means sounding confident and not asking open-ended questions. For example, don't ask questions such as, "Why won't you accept my offer?" or "Why are you being so unreasonable?" Stick to a firm, confident presentation of your offer and the reasons that support it.

5. What is Alternative Dispute Resolution (ADR)?

Alternative Dispute Resolution or ADR is a way to resolve a legal dispute outside of the traditional court system. In other words, it is an alternative to litigation. It is typically less formal than court and is usually confidential. Besides negotiation (discussed earlier), mediation is the most common form of ADR that I have encountered as an alternative to duking it out in the courtroom.

5.1 Mediation

Mediation is a process where a third party (the mediator) helps the parties to work through their dispute. The goal is for the parties to come to an agreement together. It is a voluntary process and the mediator does not make the decision. Instead, the mediator will use dispute resolution techniques to guide the parties to points of intersection and agreement. When you're stuck in the same loop of your position versus the other side's position, mediators are amazing at unlocking what looks like a hopeless situation.

What happens if mediation doesn't work? You simply go back to where you were before mediation commenced. While you lose the time and money you put into the mediation, you may have moved closer to a settlement by gaining understanding of each other's points of view and what the issues are. In my experience, mediation is a very valuable tool and usually worth trying.

Mediation may be offered through the courts or a nonprofit agency at a reduced cost or for free. Otherwise, the parties typically split the costs of mediation equally; however, you may be able to negotiate a different arrangement with the other side.

You may hear that some cases are not suited for mediation. That can be true in some cases involving significant power imbalances or a history of violence such as domestic abuse. A capable mediator will be able to identify power imbalances and often can put tools in place to even the playing field.

If you are concerned about a power imbalance making mediation unfair, the question to ask yourself is whether you are able to sit down at a table with a mediator to try to work out a solution with the other side and, if the process is not working, whether you would be able to tell the mediator that mediation is not working and that you would like to end the mediation. (Usually the other side is present in the room, but in cases where there is a power imbalance or a history of abuse the mediator may separate the parties and "shuttle" back and forth between them.)

If you are considering mediation, I recommend that you raise any concerns you have with a potential mediator. Because the process is voluntary you can always walk away from the table.

Mediators do not have to be lawyers. Some have prior experience in social work or with the justice system. However, many mediators are lawyers. Licensing requirements vary from jurisdiction to jurisdiction and, in fact, in some jurisdictions there is no formal licensing requirement. I recommend finding a mediator who belongs to a professional organization of mediators that has training requirements and professional conduct rules.

If you hire a lawyer as a mediator, he or she will set aside his or her lawyer hat and just be a mediator. That means he or she should not give you or the other side legal advice. An advantage to your mediator also being a lawyer is that he or she can bring legal training to the drafting of any settlement agreement. As well, a lawyer's familiarity with the law and, if they are also a litigator, their experience with court, are advantages.

That said, many of the best mediators I have encountered are not lawyers. (I have favourite mediators because I frequently send my clients to mediation.) A skilled non-lawyer mediator will be just as able to facilitate a mediation as a skilled lawyer and will likely cost less. My rule of thumb is that if the issue in dispute involves the transfer of real estate, is related to business or complicated financial issues, or involves interpreting the law, then a lawyer-mediator is my first choice. For example, for a family law matter, issues about parenting time or about who gets what car are fine for a non-lawyer but if the case involves a pension and the potential transfer of a home, then I'd stick with a lawyer-mediator.

Mediation often costs only a fraction of the cost of a trial. Once you and the other side agree on a mediator, the mediator will ask you to sign a mediation agreement which will outline the rules for how the mediation process works.

Mediation has huge benefits and should be carefully considered as a tool for resolution. There are provincial associations of mediators which have online referral services through their websites. There may also be nonprofit organizations that offer mediation. For example, in British Columbia Mediate BC has a roster of mediators which you can search on its website, mediatebc.com.

5.2 Arbitration

Arbitration is kind of like hiring a private judge to resolve your dispute. In arbitration you hire an arbitrator to hear evidence and decide your dispute or an aspect of it. The process is less formal than a trial.

Arbitration can be a quick and easy way to resolve a dispute without the delays and without the strict procedure and evidence rules of court. Arbitration can be private and thus advantageous for people who do not want to air private grievances in public. How it works is you and the other side have to agree on an arbitrator and how he or she will get paid (yes, you have to pay the person). Arbitrators are frequently retired judges or experienced lawyers; many are also mediators. You will then sign an arbitration agreement with the arbitrator who will explain to you the rules for the arbitration. If you disagree with an arbitrator's decision, there may be rules about how to appeal that decision. The arbitrator may have a specific format for how he or she will receive evidence or may allow you and the other side to agree on how evidence will be admitted. The flexibility to design your own process in arbitration can be a significant benefit, but it is important to agree before the arbitration on how it is going to be set up.

Arbitration can be a useful way to unlock a particular issue. For example, if you are able to agree settling on most aspects of your dispute but one issue remains outstanding, you may want to hire an arbitrator to decide that issue.

The downside of arbitration is that like a trial, you do not have control over the final decision. Also, once you've started arbitration you cannot end the process unless the other side agrees (unlike with mediation). The upside is that in cases where you truly cannot find settlement it is a less time-consuming and stressful process than a trial.

5.3 Collaborative law

As with mediation, collaborative law is a voluntary process in which you and the other side work towards reaching a settlement agreement. Collaborative law does involve working with a lawyer. A principle of collaborative law is that your advocate will work collaboratively with the other side and not adversarially, as in the traditional litigation model.

You also must agree not to go to court while participating in the collaborative law process. Because collaborative law involves working with lawyers and other professions, you cannot be self-represented in the collaborative law process.

If you can afford it, collaborative law is one of the best legal tools for resolving family law disputes, and it can be made affordable when divorce coaches are used. Divorce coaches work with clients on various issues such as parenting time and charge a lower hourly rate than lawyers. Thus, ideally, the lawyer will focus on providing legal advice and do the technical work such as drafting a Separation Agreement and not spend as much time doing the social work aspect of family law nor possibly as much time negotiating, thus reducing the lawyer's fees.

5.4 Government agencies

Your dispute may fall within the jurisdiction of certain government or nonprofit agencies that can help you with that dispute. These agencies might include an ombudsman's office, provincial attorney general, consumer affairs departments, professional licensing boards (e.g., if your dispute is about the services provided by a doctor or lawyer), or a Human Rights tribunal. For example, in BC the not-for-profit corporation Consumer Protection BC can help with complaints about unfair debt collection. Because these agencies generally are free, they are a valuable resource. Be careful to research what the agency can actually do for you. Can it provide a solution that is adequate? Are you better off filing in court? If you let the agency help you, will that mean you can't later file in court? These are questions about which you ultimately may need to seek legal advice.

5.5 Do nothing

It is always an option before commencing a court case to choose simply to walk away. You should not underestimate what a relief it may be to avoid a costly and stressful legal battle. Be aware that when you do this, there may be certain deadlines (limitation periods) that may expire. You may lose your opportunity to pursue your claim. Also, your decision not to go to court doesn't mean the other side might not decide to sue you. However, if they do this, you may have the option to counter-claim (which means make claims against them).

6. Writing an Enforceable Agreement or Consent Judgment

If you have agreed on terms for a settlement with the other side, the next step is to write down those terms in a settlement agreement. If you are already involved in court, you may want or need a judge to make those terms an order of the court, which may be known as a Consent Order or Consent Judgment.

6.1 Elements of a settlement agreement

A settlement agreement between two or more parties is essentially a contract. A contract is an agreement whereby each party to the contract promises to do something in exchange for something else from the other party.

Law students spend a large amount of time in school looking at cases about contracts that have been broken or breached. We learn the essential elements of what makes a valid, enforceable contract by looking at contracts that the courts have decided do not actually work. But one thing few law schools actually teach (at least when I went to law school in the 1990s) is how to draft a contract. The way I learned (and continue to learn) is from my experience with contracts other lawyers have drafted and adopting the parts that I feel would be useful for my clients. (I also benefited from the Professional Legal Training Course which is required for all law school graduates seeking admission to the Law Society of British Columbia, and a year of apprenticeship called "articles" under the supervision of many excellent lawyers at the Legal Services Society of BC.) Many of the practice books lawyers use contain examples of Settlement Agreements. Use your local law library and ask your law librarian to see if he or she can help you find a sample.

Because this book is not specific to any one jurisdiction or area of law, I am not able to go into detail about a settlement agreement for each province and area of law that may be needed. But there are specific requirements for certain kinds of contracts which you will have to become aware of; I recommend you research what a settlement agreement needs to have in it to work in your jurisdiction and with respect to the area of laws with which you are dealing. I also recommend you try to obtain some sample agreements to look over. You should be careful that these sample agreements are both for your jurisdiction and for your area of law. Many of the online "for sale" agreements are not tailored for the right jurisdictions or areas of law.

Here are some guidelines to drawing up a clear settlement agreement:

1. Research the elements necessary in your jurisdiction and for your area of law.

2. Use a precedent (an example) from your jurisdiction and your area of law to get a general idea what the agreement should look like and what kinds of clauses are included. Do not copy that example but instead use it to generate ideas about the form and content of your agreement.

3. Start with the agreed-upon facts. This first part of a settlement agreement is often called the preamble. It is meant to provide background information to a person who is picking up the document for the first time so it can be understood. For example, this is where you would describe who the parties are. The facts should tell a simple story that provides context to why the agreement is being made and why the particular terms are reasonable.

4. Include the terms. This is the part of the agreement whereby you and the other party agree to do certain things. It is essential that you are as specific as possible with the terms in this section. Each term should clearly indicate who, what, where and when as closely as possible.

5. Concluding clauses will depend on your jurisdiction and the nature of the agreement. Common concluding language standard to many agreements include:

   • That the agreement was entered into voluntarily.

   • If the agreement is a comprehensive agreement settling all disputes between the parties, a statement releasing each party from all claims against the other party. This is known as a "release" or "general release." (Your jurisdiction may have specific laws about a release.)

- How to change the agreement. For example, if the agreement is in writing and signed before witnesses, generally it is good to state that this is also required for any new agreement modifying the agreement.

One final note: A settlement agreement could be changed by a court in certain circumstances. Courts generally do not like to do this. An exception are agreements affecting parenting issues and child support which courts may be more likely to change if there have been changes in the circumstances of the children or parties since the agreement was signed.

See the download kit included with this book for some examples of badly drafted clauses and well-drafted clauses.

6.2 Elements of a consent order

Even though a consent order is made by a judge, the parties first must agree on the terms. In other words, you and the other side must tell the judge what exactly you agreed on. A judge will then review what you propose and either approve it, not approve it, or approve it but suggest or order changes to it.

If you and the other side wish a consent order to end the legal dispute, it is important that you make that clear in the order. For example, both sides can agree on a term that dismisses each of their claims. Alternately, a term could be added that dismisses claims upon a certain event or act such as payment by a certain date. You will have to do further research or consult a lawyer in order to put together a consent order that works in your jurisdiction and with your kind of dispute.

Once the terms of an agreement have been generally agreed to, if the parties are represented, one of the lawyers will prepare a draft consent order which is then reviewed and approved by the other side's lawyer. This draft is often handed to the judge on the day a hearing has been scheduled to "speak to" the consent order. Some courts do not require attendance at a hearing unless the judge when reading the draft consent order requires further information or has concerns about the draft order. If an agreement is reached in the hallway before court and there is no time to prepare a proper, written draft, usually one of the lawyers or, if the parties are self-represented, one of them will tell the court what the terms of the order are.

If you are drafting a consent order, you should look at other consent orders so that you can use the same style. Orders are written in the voice of the Court and tell the parties what to do. For example, an order might say, "John Jones shall pay $100 to Susan Smith by certified cheque on or before March 1, 20XX."

6.3 Consent order or settlement agreement?

There are significant differences between a settlement agreement and a consent order reached by agreement. (Talking to a lawyer is a good idea.) Generally speaking, the biggest difference is often that with a settlement agreement you and the other side have created the agreement and so the two of you can agree to change it. Typically, if you want to change it, you should do it in the same manner as the first agreement. If it is in writing, changes will need to be made in a new written agreement called an Amended Settlement Agreement and signed in the same way by the same parties (e.g., if originally signed in front of witnesses, do this again, though the witnesses can be different).

A court order, on the other hand, is made by the Court. Therefore, only the Court (that is, a judge of the same court or a higher court) can change it. This means you will have to follow court procedure to go back to court. (Yes, this will be more complicated.)

The other significant difference between a settlement agreement and a court order is generally (and there are exceptions) that if one party doesn't do what the consent order says, they are in violation of a court order, not just a contract. If you want to enforce that consent order, it is frequently easier to go back to the Court that made the order and ask the Court to make the other party do what they were supposed to do rather than to start an action for enforcement of a contract. In situations involving breach of a settlement agreement or a court order, it is best to talk to a lawyer, especially if you want to use some of the legal tools available that can make a party pay money they were supposed to pay.

2
Learning the Law

This chapter is intended to steer you toward the resources that will help you gain an understanding of the relevant law for your case.

Nowadays, access to legal resources is at an all time high; in fact, there is so much out there that your first task will be to filter out the information that does not apply and to start working through a relevant, useful, and up-to-date website or book.

That being said, I cannot recommend highly enough the value of consulting with a lawyer early on not only to learn what laws apply to your situation but, more importantly, to get an opinion as to whether you have a good case or not. Even a one-off consultation with a lawyer can give you huge advantages:

1. Knowledge of the relevant law both general (does your family law dispute also involve a non-family law element such as a potential criminal charge?) and specific (is there a regulation that explains and clarifies a particular statute section?).

2. Knowledge from someone with practical experience in the courts. Lawyers are in court all the time. They have the best sense of what will happen with your case if you do push forward and litigate. For example, in my experience the courts can vary from city to city in terms of how they deal with certain cases

as well as from judge to judge. The law might be the same but there is a certain amount of wiggle room a judge has between what facts he or she believes and how he or she interprets the relevant law. Talking to a lawyer who knows the court and the potential judges you may end up with can offer you valuable insight. Judges are human and lawyers often have insight on the best way to present a case to a specific judge.

3. They can advise you if there are any steps you need to immediately take so you don't miss out on the opportunity to bring your claim. For example, in British Columbia most civil matters have a two-year window from the date of the wrong doing to start a claim. However, if you want to start a provincial Human Rights Complaint, you need to start your claim within six months.

1. Overview of Where Law Comes From

Canada (with the exception of provincial law in Quebec) is known as a common law jurisdiction. In common law jurisdictions, the courts interpret laws that are made by the legislature. They make decisions that are binding on lower courts in the same jurisdiction so that a lower court must apply the law in the same way as a higher court for similar factual scenarios. Thus, a decision by the BC Court of Appeal is binding on decisions made by the BC Supreme Court. The decisions of the courts are known as case law. In distinction, civil law jurisdictions such as Quebec rely on codified law for non-federal matters more than case law.

There are two streams of legislated law in Canada: federal and provincial. An example of federal law is criminal law which is therefore the same across the nation. Provincial laws are made in each provincial legislature and only apply within that province. Examples of these laws include family law (except divorce, which is federal), most contract and property law, and landlord tenant law. Whether you are dealing with a provincial or a federal law should not make much of a difference in terms of the steps you need to take to become familiar with that law. One important aspect of how these laws work is that if a provincial and a federal law conflict (they tell you to do different things), the federal law trumps the provincial law. This is extremely rare and if you suspect that you are dealing with such a situation, you should talk to a lawyer.

What you want to do is find out what laws made by statute or regulation apply to the situation at hand. Your goal is to gain enough understanding to be able to know whether you have a case that is strong (in other words, more likely to win than lose). Next, you will want to check to see if the courts have any cases that have interpreted those laws in a way that is relevant to the facts in your case.

2. How to Know Which Laws Apply

There are millions of laws out there and millions of cases. How do you find the ones that apply to your specific set of facts? Even after more than 15 years of practicing law, I still approach any new area of law by starting at the most basic, simplest expression of the law. I go to resources made for self-represented litigants. I do this because these pamphlets, websites, and books explain the law in general terms and help me to quickly know what the law is. In other words, they provide the big picture. Then, I work my way up the ladder from these less complicated, more general resources to the actual laws and cases that I will need to tell the judge about. The following is the game plan I recommend.

2.1 Step one: To get a general idea of what the law is, start with resources designed for self-represented persons

Resources for self-represented people are often available through the websites of provincial legal aid agencies in your jurisdiction such as the Legal Services Society of BC. If you do not have access to the Internet, your local law library may have print copies of some of these materials. Libraries also often have free Internet access and the librarians will be able to direct you to similar resources. Courthouses may even have a pamphlet section.

I wouldn't recommend quoting these materials in court or asking the court to read them because a court does not have to follow what they say. (However, it would be fine if you used these resources as a tool to help you explain to the court what your view of the law is.) A court only has to follow what the actual law states (the legislation) and any case from a higher court that dealt with the same situation. (When your facts match up with a case from a higher court the higher case's decision is said to be "on point" and the case is said to be a "precedent.")

Web-based resources that explain the law for *pro se* litigants may be sufficient if your case does not involve a complicated legal issue or for purposes of negotiating a settlement. If the issue is more complicated, and a trial or a hearing is looking likely, then move on to step two.

How do you know if an issue is complicated? For self-represented persons, any set of facts may be overwhelming when considering how the law applies to them. So, what might in fact be a very simple issue with a straightforward answer might look more difficult than it really is. While the best way to really get a handle on this is to sit down with a lawyer, simple issues can generally be summarized in just one or two sentences. For example, if you are the parent of a minor child, in many jurisdictions you will have a duty to pay child support if the child does not live primarily with you. The law clearly applies to the facts. However, once you start parsing out the meaning of words like "parent" (let's say the child is your step-child) and asking about who the child really lives with (let's say that you share parenting time with the other side roughly equally), and if you are uncertain about what your income really is because you are self-employed and it fluctuates, then that simple issue isn't simple anymore. Suddenly, one or two sentences are multiplying into a series of paragraphs. That's a complicated issue.

2.2 Step two: Use the resources lawyers use

I have practiced law in a few different jurisdictions over my career. In each jurisdiction, I used manuals that lay out what the law is for lawyers. Often they have titles such as Family Law Resource Manual or Divorce Law Basics, or Personal Injury Resource Manual, or Personal Injury Practice and Procedure. These manuals are typically produced by the Continuing Legal Education (CLE) organization for the province. (In BC that organization is called the Continuing Legal Education Society of British Columbia or CLEBC.) These manuals are available in courthouse libraries. Though they are written for lawyers, there is no reason why a non-lawyer cannot use them. Also, for example in BC, the materials articled students use to study for the bar exam are available online through the Professional Legal Training Course (PLTC) and offer a helpful overview of the law for many subject areas.

Legal manuals will usually quote relevant law and the relevant cases. Make notes of these; you may need to refer to them during your trial. For now, however, the goal is simply to get a sense of whether your case is good or not. Generally, the standard to win a civil case is "on a balance of probabilities." This means that a judge or jury will be more likely than not to find your claims successful. In other words, you need to tip the balance more than 50 percent. That means the judge might have some doubts about your claims but are more likely to believe you and your witnesses than the other side.

2.3 Step three: Go to the statutes

The resources in steps one and two likely will have explained and referred you to the applicable statues and, if there are any, regulations. (Statutes are made and passed by the legislature. Regulations, on the other hand, are made by government agencies that administer those laws.) In preparation for trial, you will want to have copies of these laws.

How do you read a statute? Finding the right statutes can be difficult. You should look for two types of invaluable resources. The first is a compilation of statutes and regulations on a particular area in one book. For example, in BC, every year there is an updated BC Family Law and Legislation book that includes all relevant family law statutes and annotations to them. The annotations explain the laws in a very helpful manner. The second resource for black letter law (as statutes are known) is online. For example, www.canlii.org has a vast array of Canadian statutes and regulations. Another good place to start is Povnet.ca.

If there is an index for a particular statute, start there. Get a sense of the entire act or area of law. As you hone in on one section, there may be other sections that say that the section you are relying on doesn't apply in situations such as yours.

Warning: When doing legal research, it is important to make sure whatever resource you are using is up to date, because the law may have changed. The legislature may have amended the statute you are relying on or a recent case may also have changed the way the courts have to interpret the law or even decided the law is unconstitutional. With statutes, check online for the most recent version of the law. For cases, see section 2.4, Step four: Case law and the courts.

What is the difference between a statute and a regulation? Statutes are laws made by the legislature, either the Provincial Legislature or the Federal House of Commons.

The legislature can delegate some of the fine tuning or administration of the laws to government organizations who make regulations. The purpose is for government to more easily be able to adapt aspects of the law to changing times without having to go through the time-consuming approval process for amending a law in the legislature. If a statute and a regulation conflict (that is, tell you different things), the statute trumps the regulation.

2.4 Step four: Case law and the courts

If your case is relatively straightforward, knowing the applicable legislation may be all you need. But if your case is complicated, you may need to look further: The written decisions of the courts in your jurisdiction. In other words, case law.

There are rules about the way cases and statute are written down and referred to in court. This is known as citing a law or case. For example, the case *Moge v. Moge*, a leading case on spousal support, is cited as *Moge v. Moge* [1992] 3 S.C.R. 813. The parties' names are listed first, followed by the year of the decision and where the book with the case in it can be found: volume 3 of the Supreme Court Reporter, page 813.

The court system is hierarchal. That means that the top court in a jurisdiction can essentially tell lower courts how to interpret a law. A decision that interprets a law in that jurisdiction from a higher court is generally binding on a lower court. That means that if the facts and circumstances in a case at, say, the Court of Appeal in your jurisdiction, are the same as your case in the trial court, your judge will have to apply the law in your case in the same way as was done at the Court of Appeal. However, if your facts are very different, you can argue that the case is distinguishable and thus not binding on the lower court. Make sense? The long and short of it is a higher court tells a lower court how to follow the law when the facts are similar.

The old-fashioned way to find case law is to go to a law library where you'll find large volumes of reports from your jurisdiction's higher courts. The volumes will stretch from floor to ceiling and you basically need a law or librarian's degree to find anything in them. Fortunately, law libraries often have librarians in them. With a librarian's help you should be able to find some relevant cases (hopefully that you already have citations for from legal textbooks). Law librarians used to write very neatly in the margins the names of cases that quoted the case or overturned it.

But it's the 21st century. Not many lawyers use these volumes of cases anymore. I probably haven't gone to a law library and looked in a case reporter volume since the 1990s (and only then as we had to learn how to do so in law school). Today, lawyers find cases through mostly private legal database companies.

The two primary legal resources for cases in Canada are Quicklaw and Westlaw. They are often available for free at courthouse libraries.

After Quicklaw and Westlaw, CanLii.org, the website for the Canadian Legal Information Institute is an excellent resource. If I don't have access to Quicklaw or Westlaw, this is where I go. In fact, it is so easy to use I sometimes just go right to CanLII.

There are hundreds of cases out there and there may be hundreds of decisions interpreting a law that you need to research. A useful trick is to start with the most recent cases. Often a judge's written decision will contain a summary of the relevant law, explaining how the law developed to the present day and thus provide you with a history of relevant cases. It will also often provide a clear explanation of the law. (Be careful of cases that have been overturned on appeal. If a Court of Appeal decision was appealed and the higher court, for example, the Supreme Court of Canada, struck down that decision and said that the law was not correctly interpreted, then that Court of Appeal decision should not be used because it has no precedential value. Overturned decisions are bad law.)

What about cases that are not binding? Cases from the same level of court may still have what is known as persuasive value. So, for example, if you find a case from the BC Supreme Court and you are about to have a trial in that same court, your judge does not have to follow what that same court has done before. However, your judge may find that knowing how another judge decided the case may help him or her to decide the case. (It makes the judge's job easier because you are showing the judge that what you are suggesting he or she do has been done before and you are handing him or her a case as a sort of blueprint.) Sometimes a court will look at a case from another jurisdiction (e.g., from another province or, more rarely, from another country), often if the case if from a higher court such as a Court of Appeal, for persuasive reasons. Persuasive cases can never be used to persuade a judge to go against the law of your jurisdiction. However, in cases where the law is not clear, they can be very helpful in moving a judge closer to your position.

3. How to Read a Case

First, let me say that it is not easy to read and understand a legal case. Most of them are dull and full of legal jargon. Lawyers get used to the way cases are written in their first year of law school. But that first year is not easy and I remember desperately trying to understand what each case was all about. I ordered a book of summaries of the top cases and attended optional tutorials even though I'd studied philosophy and English literature in my undergraduate studies, I found the long-winded cases, which had no plot and no real characters, just "parties," hard to grasp. I adopted a multipronged approach which seemed to work. I'd read what a legal manual had to say about the case, then I'd read the "head note." A head note is a summary of the case that is often (but not always) put at the beginning of the case. (It's not actually part of the case though.)

I'd also look at the way other cases applied the case. From these different angles I was able to hone in on what was actually important in the case. Often among hundreds of sentences, it was only one. That is why I do recommend using legal manuals to help you understand a case. It might be one sentence that is quoted in a legal manual from a case that is all you need to get a sense of what the law is and what you should tell the judge.

Generally, when a judge writes a decision he or she does the following:

1. Provides an overview of the facts.

2. States what the law is.

3. Makes an application of the law to the facts.

4. Provides a conclusion (otherwise known as, the decision).

What you want to hone in on first is, number one. Are the facts in the case you are reading similar to your case? If so, the case is on point. If not, the case is "distinguishable" (another word for different). The next thing is to look at what the law is.

As I've noted above, cases contain very useful summaries of the law. They also refer to other cases, which you might find useful. Take note of how the judge applies the law to the facts. This is what you will be doing when you make a closing argument. The way cases are written can provide you with a good example of how your closing argument at trial should be made.

3
Filing in Court

Filing in court is the first step to starting a court case. The other side won't know about the case, however, until they are "served." This means that they are given the filed court papers in the manner required by Court Rules such as by a process server. Then, if the other side wishes to participate in and defend the case that person will also file court papers, which will have to be served on the person who started the case.

This chapter first looks at what steps the person who starts a court case (the plaintiff) should take. Next, it looks at what the person who is served with court papers (the defendant) should do. Whether plaintiff or defendant, I recommend that you understand what the other side has to do and read the entire chapter.

The final part of this chapter recommends organizing your litigation file. Staying on top of your papers and having what you need at your fingertips is half the battle in litigation. Lawyers are organized and, if you want to win your case, you'll need to be too.

1. Where Do I Start? Plaintiff's Perspective

First of all, a plaintiff (that is, a person who is starting a court case) will need to determine what court has jurisdiction over the case. When a court has jurisdiction it means essentially two things:

1. That the case fits into the geographic area that the court handles. For example, you cannot file suit against a supermarket in a slip-and-fall case in Saskatchewan if the store and you are based in British Columbia.

2. That a court has the authority to handle the kind of case you have. For example, in British Columbia you cannot file for a divorce in Provincial Court (though you can file for other family law issues related to divorce such as child support). If you try to file in the wrong court, the registry staff at the courthouse may not accept the case for filing or, if they mistakenly do, a judge might dismiss the case once there is a hearing or, if you are lucky, transfer the case to the correct court.

A court's authority to handle a certain kind of case is generally given to that court by statute. If you have identified which area of law applies to your case (see Chapter 2: Learning the Law), you may already know which court handles your dispute.

The rules of court for each province will contain the rules for each particular court and sometimes for each area of law. For example, BC Supreme Court has its own rules for civil disputes (e.g., a contract dispute) which are different from the BC Supreme Court's rules for family law cases, the BC Supreme Court Family Rules.

If there is a courthouse in your community that handles the area of law your dispute is about, you should go to that courthouse itself and confirm at the registry window where to file disputes of the type you have. You should also look over the Court Rules for the court that has jurisdiction. Sometimes you have to sue where an accident occurred, sometimes you have to sue in the jurisdiction where you (or the defendant) reside, and sometimes you have to sue where a contract was signed. It will depend on the area of law and the jurisdiction that handles your kind of dispute.

Note that sometimes you may have a choice of court. For example, in cases where the amount of damages you are seeking is close to the limit for small claims court, you may want to lower the amount of damages you ask for so that you can file in easier-to-use small claims court rather than trial court.

So, let's say you want to sue someone for $30,000; in BC the Small Claims ceiling is $25,000. Because suing in Supreme Court would be more complicated you may want to choose to only sue for $25,000. Also, in BC family law disputes about child support or parenting time often may be filed in either BC Supreme Court or BC Provincial Court.

If you have a choice of court, you should seek advice about the pros and cons of each court before filing.

1.1 What gets filed?

Once you've found the right registry, ask if it has *pro se* forms for self-represented people or a guide on how to file a claim for your particular issue. Often, courts will have a do-it-yourself claim form for you to fill in. The claim you eventually file in court may be called a Statement of Claim, Notice of Claim, Complaint, Application to Obtain an Order, Plaintiff's Claim, or other similar name. (I will call this document a Statement of Claim for ease of reference.)

1.2 Who are the parties?

Who are you suing or defending yourself against? Is it more than one person? Is there someone else on your side? Determining who the parties are to a lawsuit is critical.

For example, in a contract dispute, you (the plaintiff) might decide to sue the person who performed the work on your home (the defendant). But what if that person was an employee of a business? If you failed to name the business with whom you had a contract, your case might be dismissed. If someone else suffered a loss in the same incident that you are suing about (for example, your spouse and you contracted to have a home renovation which was not completed), that person (your spouse) can also be a plaintiff (or "claimant," "applicant," or such other term as the jurisdiction you are in uses for the person suing another person) with you. It is often wise to cast the net widely and sue all possible defendants so that, when it is time to enforce a winning judgement, you will have a better chance of finding those pockets that are not empty.

Other types of possible parties are legal entities (not real human beings) such as a partnership, corporation, city, or province. It is critical that you spell the full name of the persons or other entities correctly. If you misname them, it will be difficult to change the court papers later (it will likely cost you filing fees again) and make enforcing a judgement (i.e., getting your money) very difficult. So, always get the names you are suing right. (The court you are filing in may have specific rules about this.)

If the person or entity you are suing uses different names (e.g., Lou Smith, Louis Smith, or Louie Smith) it is best to use all the names they are known by in the claim. To do so you would add "also known as" or "a.k.a." after what you believe to be their legal name or the name they use most often (thus: Louis Smith a.k.a., Lou Smith a.k.a., Louie Smith).

If suing a business, there may be specific rules about how to do so in your jurisdiction. It is prudent to find out who owns a business and sue that person too. (This is not necessarily true for corporations, however.) Finding out who stands behind a business is usually not difficult.

1.3 How do I write my claim?

Your filed claim will likely be the Court's — that means your judge's — first impression of your case. During your trial you will have to stick to the claim that you made in your Statement of Claim. That means you can't just add a new claim to what you want on the day of trial. For example, if you did not claim alimony in your filed divorce claim, you cannot add it to your claims in the middle of your trial. If you do leave out a claim and later wish to add it, you will have to file an amended claim. Read your jurisdiction's court rules carefully if you do decide to file an amended claim. You might need a judge's permission. Great care should be made to get your initial Statement of Claim right.

A little-known fact about lawyers: They recycle parts of their favourite documents. A well-written legal document is something a lawyer will save as a template, tailoring it each time to the facts of each unique case. This means using the form and some of the legal language of a template but being very careful to not reuse the facts. Vet any templates you find online or elsewhere carefully as they may come from outside your jurisdiction (not helpful and potentially misleading) or be for a very different lawsuit. The most helpful template will come from the court you are filing in or from a legal aid website for cases such as yours. Ask the court if it has a sample Statement of Claim for you to look at.

If you are able to obtain a template, I recommend not typing into a template or cutting and pasting from one but rather using it as a guide to write your Statement of Claim from scratch. This is because you might cut and paste language you do not understand or does not belong.

Your written claim should be clear, accurate, and concise. The basic structure of a Statement of Claim is pretty standard. You are going to tell the Court:

1. What happened (the facts); only include "material facts." These are facts that prove your claims. Keep it brief and to the point.

2. What the law says about those facts. In other words, what is the legal basis for your case?

3. What you want the court to do (sometimes called "relief," or your "remedy") against each of your named defendants.

Things not to include in your Statement of Claim:

1. Evidence: Generally you do not need to attach documents or information that supports your case to the Statement of Claim. Your opportunity to introduce that information will be at a hearing. (There are exceptions to this rule such as some administrative law proceedings.)

2. Information that does not support your claim: There is no need for information that does not support your claim. You might feel that "background" information will help the court. However, all the court generally will need is enough information to understand who the parties are.

3. General, nonspecific information: Do not guess or theorize. Set out the facts. For example, do not write, "I believe the Defendant did X, Y, and Z." If it is a fact write, "The Defendant did X, Y, and Z."

In an ideal court system, a Statement of Claim and a Reply would contain a simple but accurate explanation of the facts, the law and what the parties want the Court to do. Typically, cases in Small Claims courts are just that simple. However, in cases that are not in Small Claims the simple facts sometimes get mixed into a smorgasbord of legal jargon. Knowing when to use this jargon can be very tricky but important. Thus it is essential for you to not only know the law and the court procedure but also to look at and consider examples of what a typical Statement of Claim or Reply looks like and what wording is used for cases similar to yours.

Sample 1 is an example of a motor vehicle Statement of Claim and a Reply for the same case. (Note that Sample 1 is based on a case in British Columbia. It is for information only. You should look for samples in your jurisdiction and for the type of case you have. Do not copy or use this sample.) As you can see, the Statement of Claim contains a bare bones recital of the facts but also a litany of legalese and standard (boiler plate) language used in most vehicle claims. The reply is focused on using legal language to deny, deny, deny.

Sample 1
Statement of Claim and Reply

No. _____

Victoria Registry

In the Supreme Court of British Columbia

Between:

Jennifer Jones

Plaintiff

and:

Elliott Smythe

Defendant

NOTICE OF CIVIL CLAIM

This action has been started by the Plaintiff(s) for the relief set out in Part 2 below.

If you intend to respond to this action, you or your lawyer must:

(a)   file a response to civil claim in Form 2 in the above-named registry of this court within the time for response to civil claim described below, and

(b)   serve a copy of the filed response to civil claim on the Plaintiff.

If you intend to make a counterclaim, you or your lawyer must:

(a)   file a response to civil claim in Form 2 and a counterclaim in Form 3 in the above-named registry of this court within the time for response to civil claim described below, and

(b)   serve a copy of the filed response to civil claim and counterclaim on the Plaintiff and on any new parties named in the counterclaim.

JUDGEMENT MAY BE PRONOUNCED AGAINST YOU IF YOU FAIL to file the response to civil claim within the time for response to civil claim described below.

Time for response to civil claim

A response to civil claim must be filed and served on the Plaintiff(s) —

(a)   if you were served with the notice of civil claim anywhere in Canada, within 21 days after that service;

(b)   if you were served with the notice of civil claim anywhere in the United States of America, within 35 days after that service;

(c)   if you were served with the notice of civil claim anywhere else, within 49 days after that service; or

(d)   if the time for response to civil claim has been set by order of the court, within that time.

CLAIM OF THE PLAINTIFF

Part 1: STATEMENT OF FACTS

1. The Plaintiff, Jennifer Jones, (the "Plaintiff"), Massage Therapist, resides at 12 Pembroke Terrace, Victoria, British Columbia.

2. The Defendant, Elliott Smythe, (the "Defendant"), software engineer, resides at 1325 Cadbora Bay Avenue, Victoria, British Columbia.

3. On May 3, 20XX, at approximately 8:30 a.m., the Plaintiff was travelling west on Yates Street by bicycle on her way to work. She was travelling at approximately 15 kilometres per hour in the bicycle lane. The Plaintiff was wearing a neon green safety vest and bicycle helmet with reflectors.

4. At the same time and on the same date, the Defendant was driving a silver Toyota Prius on Yates Street travelling west in the lane immediately adjacent to the bicycle lane.

5. As the Plaintiff approached the intersection of Fort St. and Cook St., the light was green. The Plaintiff entered the intersection. The Defendant also entered the intersection overtaking and passing the Plaintiff and then turning right onto Cook Street. The Defendant did not signal a right turn. The right side of the Defendant's vehicle struck the Plaintiff (the "Collision") causing her to veer into the sidewalk and fall off her bicycle.

6. As a result of the Collision, the Plaintiff has suffered personal injuries causing shock, pain and suffering, loss of earnings, loss of future earning capacity, loss of housekeeping capacity, loss of past and future care, loss of insurability, loss of opportunity and loss of amenities of life. In particular, without limiting the generality of the foregoing, the Plaintiff has suffered:

    (a) injury to wrist;

    (b) injury to left leg;

    (c) such further and other injuries as the Plaintiff may advise.

7. The injuries, loss and damage have caused and continue to cause the Plaintiff pain, suffering, loss of enjoyment of life, permanent physical disability, and loss of earnings, past and prospective. All of the injuries, loss and damage were caused or contributed to by the negligence of the Defendant.

8. As a result of the said Collision, the Plaintiff has incurred expenses and suffered special damages, the particulars of which will be proven at the trial of this action.

Part 2: RELIEF SOUGHT

1. General damages against the Defendant for pain and suffering;

2. Loss of income, both past and future;

3. Costs of past and future care;

4. Loss of earning capacity;

Sample 1 — Continued

5. Special damages against the Defendant;

6. Costs against the Defendant;

7. Interest pursuant to the *Court Order Interest Act* R.S.B.C. 1996, c. 79; and

8. Such further and other relief as this Honourable Court may deem just and meet.

Part 3: LEGAL BASIS

1. The said Collision and the resulting damage, loss, expense and injury sustained by the Plaintiff were caused solely by the negligence of the Defendant, particulars of which negligence are as follows:

   a. In failing to keep a proper careful lookout for traffic, and in particular the bicycle which the Plaintiff was operating;

   b. In failing to keep the said motor vehicle under proper or any control;

   c. In driving the said motor vehicle in a negligent manner and at an excessive, dangerous and unlawful rate of speed;

   d. In driving the said motor vehicle on a road, street, or highway, when his ability to do so was impaired by alcohol, drugs, and/or fatigue;

   e. In failing to apply his brakes so as to bring the motor vehicle driven by him to a complete stop, or to slow the speed of the motor vehicle driven by him so as to avoid losing control, or alternatively, driving with defective brakes;

   f. In operating a motor vehicle when not medically fit to do so;

   g. In driving a mechanically defective motor vehicle;

   h. In failing to yield the right of way;

   i. In failing to drive the said motor vehicle in a careful and prudent manner, having regard to all the circumstances, including the rate of speed, weight, and size of the motor vehicle, the nature, use and condition of the highway, street and road, and the condition of visibility pertaining at the time, and the traffic including bicycle traffic which actually was on the roadway and which might reasonably have been expected to be there at that time, so as not to endanger himself or the safety of others;

   j. In failing to observe traffic warning lights and signs;

   k. In operating the said motor vehicle, in a reckless, careless and inexperienced manner without regard, whatsoever, for bicycles which could reasonably be expected to be on the said roadway;

   l. In driving his motor vehicle on the highway, street or road without due care and attention, or without reasonable consideration for other persons using the roadway in contravention of Section 144 of the *Motor Vehicle Act*, R.S.B.C. 1996, Chapter 318, and amendments thereto;

   m. In failing to take any or sufficient action to avoid the collision.

[Omitted concluding part of form includes addresses for service and of the registry and signature of plaintiff.]

Sample 1 — Continued

No. _____

Victoria Registry

In the Supreme Court of British Columbia

Between:

Jennifer Jones

Plaintiff

and:

Elliott Smythe

Defendant

RESPONSE TO CIVIL CLAIM

Filed by: Elliott Smythe (the "Defendant")

Part 1: RESPONSE TO NOTICE OF CIVIL CLAIM FACTS

Division 1 – Defendant's Response to Facts

1.   The facts alleged in paragraph 2 of Part 1 of the notice of civil claim are admitted.

2.   The facts alleged in paragraphs 3, 4, 5, 6, 7, and 8 of Part 1 of the notice of civil claim are denied.

3.   The facts alleged in paragraph 1 of Part 1 of the Notice of Civil Claim are outside the knowledge of the Defendant.

Division 2 – Defendant's Version of Facts

1.   The Defendant says that if there was a collision between a motor vehicle owned and driven by the Defendant and the Plaintiff's bicycle, as alleged in paragraph 5 of part 1 of the Notice of Civil Claim, the Plaintiff sustained no injury, loss, damage, or expense as a result of the said collision.

2.   The Defendant says that at the time of the collision, the Plaintiff:

     (a)   was riding or operating a bicycle on a highway contrary to the provisions of s. 183 of the *Motor Vehicle Act,* R.S.B.C. 1996, c.318, and amendments thereto;

Sample 1 — Continued

(b)　was riding or operating a bicycle on a highway without due care and attention or without reasonable consideration for others using the highway;

(c)　failed to keep any, or, in the alternative, an adequate lookout;

(d)　failed to take reasonable or any precaution to avoid the collision;

(e)　failed to keep the bicycle under proper or any control;

(f)　was operating the bicycle when her ability to do so was impaired by alcohol, drugs, fatigue, illness, or any combination thereof;

(g)　was operating the bicycle without any, or in the alternative, with defective brakes, or, in the further alternative, failed to apply the brakes of the bicycle in time to avoid the said collision;

(h)　failed to avoid the collision or failed to alter the course of the bicycle to prevent the collision when the same was, or should have been, imminent;

(i)　was operating the bicycle without proper care and attention having regard to the time and place of the accident, the climatic conditions, the nature of the roadway, the traffic that was on the roadway, the mechanical condition of the bicycle and her own physical and mental condition, and the Defendant pleads and relies on the provisions of the *Negligence Act*, R.S.B.C. 1996, c.333.

Division 3 – Additional Facts

1.　The Defendant says that the acts or omissions of the Defendant were not the proximate cause of any alleged loss suffered by the Plaintiff, and further alleges that any injuries, conditions, or disabilities from which the Plaintiff has suffered since May 3, 20XX, were caused or contributed to by injuries, conditions, or disabilities which existed prior to that date, or were caused by subsequent events unrelated to the motor vehicle accident of May 3, 20XX.

2.　The Defendant says that the Plaintiff has failed to mitigate any damages she may have suffered, either as alleged in the notice of civil claim or at all, which is not admitted but specifically denied, and in particular failed to resume employment as soon as it was practicable for her to do so and has failed to follow reasonable and appropriate medical advice which, if followed, would have speeded her rehabilitation and recovery.

Sample 1 — Continued

3.   In further answer to the whole of the notice of civil claim, the Defendant says that she is a designated defendant pursuant to the provisions of s.95 of the *Insurance (Vehicle) Act*, R.S.B.C. 1996, c.231 and the Plaintiff's entitlement to recovery of loss of income is limited by the provisions of s.98 of the *Insurance (Vehicle) Act*, R.S.B.C. 1996, c. 231, and the Regulations thereto, and the defendant specifically pleads and relies upon sections 95 and 98 of the *Insurance (Vehicle) Act* R.S.B.C., 1996, c.231, and the Regulations thereto.

4.   The Defendant says that at all times material to this action the Plaintiff was insured by a Certificate of Insurance under which the Plaintiff was provided with accident benefits, coverage for medical expenses, rehabilitation expenses, and weekly disability benefits and to the extent of such benefits, which the Plaintiff has received or was entitled to receive, the Defendant says that the Plaintiff has released her claim against the Defendant by virtue of s. 83 of the *Insurance (Vehicle) Act,* R.S.B.C. 1996, c.231, as amended.

Part 2: RESPONSE TO RELIEF SOUGHT

1.   The Defendant opposes the granting of relief sought in paragraphs 1 to 8 of Part 2 of the notice of civil claim.

Part 3: LEGAL BASIS

1.   Any injury, loss, damage, or expense allegedly sustained by the Plaintiff could have been prevented, or the severity thereof reduced, if the Plaintiff had not been negligent in respect to her own personal safety and this Defendant pleads the provisions of the *Negligence Act*, R.S.B.C. 1996, c.333, and amendments thereto.

2.   The Defendant says that the onus of proof of injury and loss is on the Plaintiff.

[Omitted concluding part of form; signatures, etc.]

You will have to research to what degree your court filings will require more or less legalese and boilerplate (see the sample or a small claims court case). Note that motor vehicle cases are often taken by lawyers on a contingency-fee basis. This means they get paid only if the case wins or settles. I recommend you speak to a lawyer before filing or defending this kind of case.

Preserving the Status Quo

"Status quo" means the current state of things. When you file a lawsuit there may be some urgency to keep things as they are before the trial. For example, if you are in a business partnership and your partner has just listed business property for sale, it might not do you any good if the property is sold and the proceeds spent before trial. If that is the case, you may need to consider making an urgent motion to the court to preserve the status quo at the same time as you file your case. See Chapter 6 for motions. In property disputes or family law cases in BC, you may also want to consider filing a certificate of pending litigation (CPL) on any real estate property owned solely by the other side but which is part of the lawsuit. A CPL (sometimes called a "lis pendens") is a notice placed on the title at the land registry that informs prospective purchasers that there is litigation concerning the property. There may also be other ways to protect property. For example, in British Columbia, if you are married, you can apply under the *Land (Spouse Protection) Act* for an entry against title to the family home which should stop the property from being sold without your consent, subject to certain limitations.

2. Where Do I Start? Defendant's Perspective

If you have been served with a lawsuit, you likely have a certain number of days to file a written Defence (which also may be known by another name such as an Answer, Reply, or Response) and to serve it on the plaintiff. For example, in British Columbia if you are served with an Application to Obtain an Order in Provincial Court, you must file your Reply (defence) within 30 days of being served. If you do not file a defence, the court may assume that you agree with the claims against you. You likely will not receive any further notices from the court including the date for any hearing. Because the court will assume that you are not participating in the hearing, the court will likely give the plaintiff what he or she is asking for. A default judgement may be issued against you. This is a judgement in favour of the plaintiff because the defendant has not filed a defence or has not shown up at court. Generally, a Statement of Claim will say on it whether you are required to file a defence or if you are simply required to show up on a hearing date.

In order to file a defence, you first figure out when it must be filed and when it must be served. Often that information is written on the Statement of Claim or other papers you have been served. Then you should contact the court registry at which the lawsuit was filed in order to find out if there is a prescribed form for your defence. You might also be able to figure this out on the court's website or at a law library.

What If You Are Past the Limitation Date to File a Defence?

You may not have been able to file your defence in time. If that is the case, you should immediately contact your court registry to find out what steps are necessary to file late. In many jurisdictions, you will be required to also file a motion to ask the Court for permission to file late. The important thing to do is to prepare your defence and have it ready to file ASAP. It is usually better to file something rather than nothing. In my experience, courts prefer not to issue default judgements if there is any indication that a defendant wants to be involved in the case. If you've rushed to file your defence and later realize that you have forgotten to add certain facts or defences, you may be able to file an amended one.

Making Deals with the Other Side about Deadlines

Let's say your defence is due but you know you're not going to do a good job on it unless you spend a little more time on it. You phone the other side and ask for an extension. You agree on a new deadline. Or your defence is already late but the other side said this was fine. Is this OK? Maybe. Any agreement you reach with the other side about procedure (i.e., the Court Rules that apply in your jurisdiction about how to proceed with your case) can be changed by a judge. In other words, the Court has final say on matters of procedure. My advice to a *pro se* litigant contemplating this kind of scenario might be:

1. Try to meet all deadlines and follow your jurisdiction's Court Rules about procedure to meet any deadlines. Failure to meet a deadline, even if the other side agrees, could have severe consequences.

2. If you are going to miss a deadline, ask the other side if they would agree to an extension to a specific date.

3. If the other side agrees, contact the court registry. Explain to the clerk the agreement reached by you and the other side. Ask the local court if this is acceptable to the court, and whether permission of the court is required, and if so you should file a Consent Motion (see Chapter 6: Motions and Temporary Orders).

4. Immediately confirm your agreement with the other side by writing to the other side, spelling out the agreement.

5. When you do appear in court next, be ready to explain that you and the other side reached an agreement about a deadline and when your document was filed.

Unless you agree with everything in the Statement of Claim including if the plaintiff is asking for you to pay their filing fees and court costs, and you do not wish to participate in the court process at all, you should never ignore a Statement of Claim which is served on you. Even if you agree with the claim, it is usually a good idea to file a defence and go to any hearing date. (An exception to this would be if you dispute whether the court has jurisdiction over you in the matter at hand in which case filing and appearing in court may be deemed to waive that defence unless you make a motion to dismiss the case or specifically plead it in the defence. You should research this further or talk to a lawyer if you dispute jurisdiction.) I generally think that filing a defence in most cases is a good idea so that you can make sure that you know what is happening, to prevent the judge giving the other side court costs, and so that no surprises will happen.

A defence is similar to a Statement of Claim with one significant difference: In a defence you must deny the claims made by the plaintiff. The following are typical ingredients of a defence:

- Deny the allegations made in the plaintiff's claim with which you disagree.

- Admit the allegations made in the plaintiff's claim with which you agree.

- Provide your version of the facts that either dispute any claim made by the plaintiff or support any claim or defence you are making.

- Include what the law says about the facts. In other words, what is the legal basis for your position?

- Raise any technical problems with the plaintiff's case. For example, does the court have jurisdiction to hear this kind of case? Was the case filed within the limitation period? Were you served properly? (You may want to raise these in a motion to the court.)

- What you want the court to do (sometimes called "relief," or your "remedy"). You probably will ask for the plaintiff's claim or claims to be dismissed. Your jurisdiction may also allow you to ask for costs. (If you have counterclaims, you will ask for these.)

Typically, you will write a statement such as, "The Defendant denies the allegations of fact in paragraphs 1, 3, and 5." However, you should look at an example from your jurisdiction to see how this is typically done.

If you choose *not* to file a defence within the time limit for a defence to be filed, you may not receive any notice of court dates and a default judgement may be entered against you. In other words, the other side may get everything they have asked for without your participation.

Motion to Dismiss

There are some circumstances where you may want to ask the Court to dismiss the plaintiff's case against you before the trial because there is some technical error in the plaintiff's case. This kind of request is commonly known as a Motion to Dismiss. Motions are discussed further in Chapter 6. Common reasons for motions to dismiss include filing in the wrong court or improper service of the documents on you. To be clear, these are technical problems with the case; not just that you know the plaintiff is completely wrong. If the matter is dismissed for a technical reason, the plaintiff might be able to begin the case again.

2.1 Counterclaims

Sometimes the person you are in a dispute with files in court before you do. Or, you have claims against him or her which you only want to pursue because they are now suing you. In those cases, you (the defendant) will want to assert your claims against that person, who is now the plaintiff. To do that, you will have to add counterclaims to your defence. Most court defence forms have a place to do this. You will follow the same formula as described above for filing a claim: Lay out your facts, explain how the law applies to the facts, and tell the court what you want it to do.

You cannot counterclaim for just anything. Your counterclaims generally should relate to the same subject area as the claims against you. For example, if you have been sued for more parenting time and you counterclaim for more parenting time, a counterclaim for child support might also be in order. This is because the subject matter of the original claim, parenting time, relates to the issue of the payment of child support.

There will likely be a deadline to file any counterclaims in court and to serve them on the other side.

2.2 Adding Another Party: Cross-Claims

Let's say you receive court papers that claim you (Biker 1) were riding your bike and collided with the plaintiff (Biker 2), seriously injuring him. But in fact, it was another person (Biker 3) who collided with you and forced you to hit Biker 2. So, really, you feel it's Biker 3's fault. If you get sued by Biker 2, you will probably want to bring Biker 3 into the legal dispute.

When you bring a new party (Biker 3) into an already existing legal dispute and blame him or her for the damages, this is known as a cross-claim or cross-complaint. You will have to add the new party to your legal case according to the rules of your jurisdiction and serve him or her with the required court papers.

2.3 Filing a Claim or Defence

In order for the court to have a record of your lawsuit and to assign it a docket number, you must file it at the correct court registry. This means taking the required court papers (original plus a couple of copies) to the court registry where the registry will date-stamp them and create a new file. The registry will also give you a docket number at this time. A docket number is just a number that helps the registry find your matter. You will have to put the docket number on any future court papers you file. Depending on your jurisdiction it may be possible to mail in, fax, or efile (through the court's website). Contact the court registry beforehand to find out what forms of filing are acceptable.

3. Filing Fees

Filing fees are collected at the time of filing. These vary from court to court. If you are unable to afford the filing fee, it may be possible to have your fees waived. For example, in family cases in BC Supreme Court you can apply to ask the court for an order to waive filing fees if you receive benefits under the *Employment and Assistance Act* or the *Employment and Assistance for Persons with Disabilities Act*; or if you can't afford to pay fees without facing undue hardship.

4. Forms

There are a range of forms available to help you file your claim or defence in court. Here is a list, ranked from best to worst:

1. **Lawyer drafted:** Of course, the ideal court filing will have been drafted for you by a lawyer.

2. **Court or legal aid websites:** More and more the courts and legal aid organizations are putting up court forms including do-it-yourself tick-box forms designed for *pro se* litigants. These are useful. However, they are generic and not necessarily designed for your particular set of facts. If your case is unique, they may not cover all the areas you need. Check with the courthouse staff first to make sure the form is the right one for your case and, if possible, review the form with a lawyer to see if it is right for you. On tick-box forms there is often an area to write in extra, more unique information. You should always think about whether it is useful to use this section. Also, consider crossing out lines that are not relevant to your case. Drafting a pleading, a court order, or an agreement is critically important because these kinds of documents can impact you for a very long time.

3. **Pleading or legal manuals from a courthouse library:** Often law books have examples of legal forms and how to draft them. These may be challenging to use as they are written for lawyers.

4. **Friend's court papers:** While it might be helpful to use your friend's court papers for ideas if they were drafted by a lawyer, make sure you understand your friend's case and everything on that form before you use any of it. Do not just copy it and assume it will work for you, too.

5. **Paid online forms:** Be wary. I do not recommend using these. If not for your jurisdiction and your kind of case, these may be a waste of money.

6. **Generic online forms:** Are they for your jurisdiction? If not, they will likely be misleading and should not be used.

5. Service

The person you are suing must receive a copy of the Statement of Claim and other required forms. There are strict rules about how you send these papers to them and how you can prove to the Court that the other party actually received the documents. This is known as giving them "notice." These rules exist so that if the other side does not file a defence and does not show up for a hearing, you can be granted a "default judgement," which means the court will order the defendant to do what you have asked. Don't forget to send the Statement of Claim to **all** named defendants.

Service is the simple thing that, for me, often becomes a headache. For example, when you file a divorce in BC, personal service is required and usually you hire a process server sheriff to serve divorce papers. Typically, this costs around $100. But if the defendant lives out of province, you will have to find a process server qualified in another jurisdiction. And sometimes the defendant doesn't want to get served and decides to evade service.

One of the first divorces I ever did was on a defendant who lived in Florida. Half my time seemed to be passed researching how to serve the defendant in Florida and then, when the person was evading service, what to do so that an order could be made against him. The takeaway from this is:

1. Get service right the first time. Give whoever is serving the papers as much information about the defendant as possible including his or her address, place of work, hours at home, hours at work, what kind of car he or she drives, a physical description and, ideally, a photograph, and the defendant's cell number. If there is a problem with service (e.g., you served the defendant when a constable was required), the defendant can apply to have the whole case dismissed.

2. If you don't know where the defendant is or he or she is evading service, do a little research to try to track down the person. Maybe a mutual friend knows where the person is living and working now? Also, people do not like being served at work, generally, so telling the defendant to cooperate with the service process and be served at a location that is convenient for your process server may be in his or her interest. Depending on your kind of case, failing to get personal service and having to use alternative service (see next point below) may affect

the relief you will eventually be able to get if you cannot personally serve the defendant.

3. If you cannot serve the defendant as required by the rules for your jurisdiction, you can ask the Court for a different form of service. This is known as making a Motion for Alternate Service. You will need to show the Court that you have made your very best efforts to serve the defendant. The old-fashioned way to serve a defendant by alternate service is by publication where a notice is put in a newspaper that serves the area where the defendant last lived and to mail the papers to the defendant's last known address. Today, you can also ask for the papers to be emailed to the defendant. What the Court will be looking for in this kind of motion is both that you really tried to serve the defendant and that your alternate service has a good chance of notifying him or her. Unfortunately, alternate service is less than ideal because for some matters if actual service cannot be made, this may impact the kind of relief you are able to obtain.

6. Organization

The cornerstone of successful litigation is organization. While you might have the facts and the law on your side, they won't do you any good if you can't retrieve them from a disorganized mass of papers. I've included some useful information about organizing your litigation file on the download kit included with this book. Be sure to reference it and get your case organized.

4
Lawyers

1. Where Are the Good (Competent) Lawyers?

With respect to the quality of legal representation, let's face it, not all lawyers are created equal; or trained equally, or even willing to be mentored and get better. Some lawyers are great in court, able to keep all the facts of a case straight in their minds as they cross-examine a witness, but not so hot at drafting a complex business document. Some are superb at negotiating, somehow opening up the other side to consider options on which they completely shut you down. Others can prepare a superb legal brief, laying out the law in a way that is clear and persuasive. Some are excellent at client relations, easily building the trust relationship between lawyer and client that is the cornerstone of a successful file.

All lawyers must, however, meet a professional duty of competence. They should be pretty good at all of these skills. And most are. In my experience, a *pro se* litigant who retains a lawyer is almost always better off. If they've shopped around and go in with open eyes, my experience is that they will always be better off. (Keep in mind that even hiring a high-priced lawyer doesn't mean you'll win. Typically, a legal dispute means that there will be some form of loss, whether you have a lawyer or not. Not losing anything at all probably means you never had a legal dispute in the first place.)

2. How to Get Free (or Low-Cost) Legal Advice

Lawyers are expensive. Typical fees start at a couple of hundred dollars an hour and go up from there, and lawyers generally want some money paid up front; this is called a retainer. Retainers are usually in the thousands of dollars. Almost everything a lawyer does on your file is billable: emails, letters, research, phone calls. So, if your lawyer charges $250 an hour and sends you an email, he or she will charge you for that time. Generally, billable time is broken down into tenths. The lowest billable amount is .1, which is six minutes. So, at $250 an hour, that email will probably cost you at least $25. That's going to add up.

More and more people are going to court and representing themselves. In some courts, more than 50 percent of litigants in family law cases are self-represented. One of the main reasons litigants are going it alone is the cost of retaining a lawyer. The other, I believe, is dissatisfaction with the services lawyers provide. While it is my opinion that most lawyers provide quality services, there are some that do not and this tarnishes the reputation of all lawyers. Also, lawyers have been reluctant to offer an alternative to the traditional billable hour.

There are legal services available that are not financially onerous. It is also possible to use a lawyer's time cost effectively by managing your use of that lawyer. For instance, send the lawyer one email with ten questions instead of ten separate emails.

What's a Conflict Check?

All lawyers and organizations providing legal services must check their records to make sure professional ethical rules do not prohibit them from offering you legal services. Conflicts occur if a lawyer has, for example, represented one party and then turns around and represents the person on the other side.

Is Talking to a Lawyer Confidential?

If you consult a lawyer for legal advice, that conversation is usually confidential. You should ask the lawyer you are talking with if your meeting is confidential. (Note that there are exceptions to lawyer-client priviledge.) It will not be confidential if the lawyer is working for the other side.

2.1 Types of low- or no-cost legal assistance

2.1a Free or discounted initial consultation

Some lawyers offer a discount for a first meeting. (This first meeting is often called an "initial consultation.") You can go at any stage of the litigation though getting legal advice as soon as possible is always recommended. Check to see if the advertised discounted consultation is for a full hour or only 30 minutes. While a 30-minute consult is better than no consult, in my experience a lawyer often requires at least a full hour to be able to get the full story and to provide a legal opinion, especially if there are papers that the lawyer will have to read.

Most bar associations (e.g., Canadian Bar Association) have a lawyer referral service and many offer a discount for an initial consultation. For example, the BC Branch of the Canadian Bar Association offers an initial consultation through its referral service for $25 plus tax.

Benefits of an initial consultation:

- They are a good way to get a feel for a lawyer. You don't want a lawyer who only tells you what you want to hear, you want one who listens to you and tries to understand your goals and gives a clear opinion on what he or she thinks your chances of success are. "It could go either way" is a legitimate opinion providing the lawyer explains why this is the opinion he or she arrived at. Do you trust the lawyer?

- They are a way to get a realistic assessment of what a lawyer would charge to assist you. It is fair to ask a lawyer to estimate the cost of proceeding with your case. Ask for the cost if the case settles soon, the cost to file in court, and the cost for a trial. Usually, there is a significant escalation in cost between these three stages of litigation. You may want to hire the lawyer to prepare your documents for filing in court but then you may elect to do any motion hearings on your own but spend time consulting with the lawyer before the hearings. Will the lawyer provide limited assistance in the future and what would it cost for such services?

- Obtaining a legal opinion on your case including what constitutes a reasonable settlement offer, chances at trial, and procedural advice (i.e., What your next steps should be).

- The consultation is usually confidential.

How to prepare for an initial consultation:

1. The most important thing you can do to get the most value from your initial consultation is to sort through the documents relevant to the dispute and organize them. If there are any court orders or written agreements, put those on top and make sure the lawyer sees them.

2. Write out any questions you may have.

3. The next important thing to do is relax and show up for the meeting. If you think you might not remember all the facts, write a chronology of the relevant facts. (A chronology starts with the oldest item and works forward to the present day.) Personally, I prefer to hear a client's story directly from the client.

4. In my experience whether to bring a friend to provide you with support at the meeting is up to you. The downside to bringing someone who will not be a party in a court proceeding to a meeting with a lawyer is that the confidentiality of your meeting with the lawyer is essentially waived and, though usually unlikely, that person could be made to testify as to what happened during your meeting. (Your lawyer should meet with you separately beforehand to explain this.)

2.1b Applying for legal aid

If you are low-income, a legal aid organization may cover your kind of issue and provide you with free assistance. The application process usually requires an intake interview by a legal assistant or paralegal who will gather your relevant documents, listen to your story, and check your income. This information will be assessed to see if you are eligible for the services. Often services can range from information and/or advice to full representation.

Sometimes the legal aid organization may require you to pay filing fees and other fees (lawyers call these "disbursements"). Often, if you win court costs, you will have to surrender this to the legal aid organization. Read the retainer agreement carefully that the legal aid organization offers you. Of course, if the court orders you to pay something including court costs, these are your responsibility, not your lawyer's or legal aid's.

2.1c Applying for a pro bono lawyer

Pro bono representation can occur when you agree with a lawyer that he or she will provide free legal services. (Legal aid lawyers are paid by the legal aid organization.) Often pro bono attorneys and clients are matched through an organization that connects eligible cases with lawyers. These organizations often have similar intake procedures to legal aid; you will have an intake with a legal assistant or paralegal who will assess whether your income and your legal issue is something with which it can help you. If so, the organization will send your information to a lawyer.

Pro bono attorneys are private bar attorneys who offer volunteer services for a number of reasons: Lawyers are encouraged and sometimes required to provide a certain amount of free legal assistance every year; retired lawyers and judges enjoy giving back to the community; and sometimes lawyers want to gain experience in a new area of law.

2.1d Contingency fee

Sometimes lawyers will agree that you can pay them out of any money you receive if you settle or win your case. Typically, these fee arrangements are made in personal injury cases. Check to see what percentage the lawyer will get and also check to see who pays for additional costs such as filing fees or hiring an expert.

2.1e The pro bono or legal aid lawyers: Are they any good?

Over my career, I've been paid directly by clients (private practice), I've been a legal aid lawyer paid a fixed annual salary (or paid a fixed hourly rate by legal aid for particular cases) and I've helped people for free through pro bono organizations. In every situation, I've tried just as hard for my clients. I don't think anyone could say that my ability as a lawyer changed by how much I was paid.

I've found legal aid lawyers to usually be above-average in terms of legal skills. Often, a legal aid job is an attractive position for a good lawyer because the salary, though lower than what a lawyer may make in the private sector, is reliable. There are no non-paying clients to worry about or the risks of running a business. The opportunity to help people, especially those in need, and serve the public good can be very fulfilling. Also, legal aid lawyers work as part of a larger organization so that newer lawyers have an excellent opportunity to learn from more seasoned lawyers, many of whom are often considered experts in their field.

However, legal aid lawyers can be overworked. Though they have a professional duty to offer you competent representation, they may not have as much time to put into your case. Legal aid organizations often do not provide their lawyers with legal assistants. Thus, your lawyer will be spending time photocopying and doing other administrative tasks which means your lawyer is essentially doing two jobs. Inevitably, the care and attention that a good legal assistant can bring to your representation will be felt at some point. These factors shouldn't make or break your case, but it will mean that things may not happen as fast as you'd like. For example, a phone call may take longer to be returned or a copy of a letter may not arrive as soon as you'd like.

Sometimes lawyers who represent private clients in cases where the other side is represented by a legal aid lawyer feel that this is unfair. They claim that the legal aid represented client will refuse to settle the case because they have unlimited use of a lawyer while the represented person likely has to pay their lawyer for every phone call, every email, every letter. They say that clients with legal aid lawyers sometimes delay the case just to try to raise their legal expenses and thus grind them down. There is a grain of truth to this. (As a legal aid lawyer, I have never intentionally prolonged a case as a tactical move to force the other side pay higher legal fees.) However, when one side has unlimited access to a lawyer, be they on legal aid or be they wealthy enough to not care how high their legal fees are going, it does create an unfair playing field. The broader context is that both parties pay a price for continued litigation though the price might not be financial on the other side. Continued litigation continues stress, it makes demands on both parties' time and it continues a strategy that always carries the risk that the party may not get what they want at trial. In other words, prolonging litigation does not mean your case is any more likely to win at trial or not. As well, often a legal aid case may have restrictions on the lawyers' time. In some jurisdictions, legal aid lawyers have only a certain amount of time they can spend on a case. For example, in British Columbia private bar lawyers can take legal aid cases but are only paid for a pre-set number of hours on each case.

2.1f Limited Appearance Representation (LAR)

It may be possible for you and a lawyer to agree that the lawyer will perform certain tasks but not offer full representation. For example, you might agree that a lawyer will write a Motion for Summary Judgment and supporting affidavit but that you will appear in court and make the oral argument for that motion. Or you might hire a lawyer for a specific task such as conducting an examination for discovery. There are different names for these kinds of arrangements: unbundled legal services, discreet legal services, limited scope retainers, limited assistance representation, or limited appearance representation (LAR).

Some jurisdictions, such as BC and Ontario, have created rules for lawyers about this. What is most important is that you and your lawyer are clear about what the lawyer is doing, what the lawyer is not doing, what you are doing and what you are not doing. This should be set out in a retainer agreement though a letter from the lawyer is sufficient in some jurisdictions such as Ontario.

LAR is becoming more common. It helps to make quality but affordable legal services available and thus increases access to justice.

The disadvantage to this arrangement is that a lawyer is only parachuted in for part of a case and will lack the breadth of understanding that a lawyer gains through full representation. Thus, the product the lawyer generates may not be as strong as the product if he or she was fully representing you. Also, the strength a lawyer can provide to a case is usually not just limited to a specific task (e.g., ghostwriting a motion) but also to the peripheral tasks that might generate forward momentum on the case for settlement (e.g., serving the motion with a letter on a lawyer's letterhead that forcefully argues for a settlement). If you and the lawyer are not absolutely clear on what each is responsible for, there can be confusion created.

Ultimately, LAR can work well if you and the lawyer you've hired are each willing to put the time and effort into building a successful partnership.

3. How to Deal with a Lawyer on the Other Side

When the other side "lawyers up," it can be intimidating. The lawyer may tell you that your case is weak, that your settlement offers are totally off-base, and that he or she is going to cross-examine you aggressively during the trial. If this happens, take a breath, relax, and remember that a lawyer's job is to be an advocate for his or her client, and that client alone. If your case is actually the stronger case, the lawyer on the other side will never tell you that. (However, that lawyer should be telling his or her client that.)

Don't be deceived by nice-guy lawyers on the other side either. No matter how nice, friendly, or accommodating the lawyer on the other side is, remember his or her job is to advocate for his or her client, not you. Do not rely on the other side's legal advice or opinions without double checking with your own lawyer or doing your own research. Treat the lawyer politely and respectfully, and breathe a sigh of relief that the person isn't being a jerk, but double check (with a smile) everything he or she says.

One critical thing to remember is that the other side's lawyer cannot ever give you legal advice and is professionally required not to. He or she can, however, try to persuade you that his or her interpretation of the law is correct and yours is not. That is another reason why you should read Chapter 2: Learning the Law and make every effort to get legal advice from your own lawyer, whether that be through a courthouse duty-counsel, referral from a bar organization, or by sitting down with a paid lawyer.

Who's the boss? Lawyer or client?

I've heard too many people tell me that they took a settlement because their lawyer told them to. Lawyers don't tell you what to do. A client is always the boss. The lawyer works for the client, not the other way round. Lawyers make recommendations and offer options for their clients. But at the end of the day, it is the client who gives the lawyer "instructions" about what to do. If it feels like your lawyer is telling you what to do rather than making recommendations, it's time to have a talk with him or her and maybe even consider another lawyer.

4. How to Hire a Lawyer

Whether it is for an initial consult, to use the lawyer occasionally for limited assistance, or because you are ready to bite the bullet and have a lawyer represent you, the best way to find a good lawyer is to get a referral from someone who works with lawyers (for example, another lawyer, an accountant, or a mental health professional).

Another avenue are lawyer referral services. For example, local bar associations often have a lawyer referral phone number. These services will match your type of case with a lawyer who does those cases. However, most of these services do not screen the lawyer for ability and whether they are a good match beyond area of law. Referral services may offer a low initial consultation rate.

The experience of friends and acquaintances with lawyers can also provide helpful leads on finding a lawyer. Bear in mind that what your friend's case was about and what your case is about may be very different and how one lawyer works for one person may differ for you.

Online services that give lawyers ratings are, in my view, not helpful. (Apparently I have three stars on one site; however, as far as I can tell no one, certainly no former client, has ever reviewed me there!)

Law firm websites can provide helpful information. For example, most include a biography of each lawyer at the firm. Look that over and see what you think. If a lawyer has published articles or books on legal topics, that usually indicates some expertise, though it may not mean the lawyer can stand on his or her feet and argue well.

With respect to years of experience, some of the best lawyers can be some of the newest lawyers. Junior lawyers will also offer a lower hourly rate. One of the best ways to find an affordable and decent lawyer is to choose a seasoned lawyer's junior associate. Often, the best new lawyers spend their early years learning from a more experienced lawyer and will take questions and issues to their mentors for advice. The top experienced lawyers will often pick the top law school graduates for their juniors. A junior lawyer at a reputable firm is often the best deal you can find if you are hiring a lawyer: It's a two for one because you get the benefits of both a fresh, energetic new lawyer and, if that junior lawyer is wise and works closely with the more experienced lawyers at the firm, the wisdom and experience of a seasoned lawyer.

You can also (and should) look the lawyer up on the Law Society or bar licensing website which will tell you if the lawyer has been found to have committed professional misconduct.

Once you've got a few names on your list, you're ready for the next step: Picking one for an initial consult.

Treat your first meeting with a lawyer as a job interview. You're the one hiring after all. You should feel like the lawyer is a good fit for you. That doesn't mean that he or she will tell you everything you want to hear. Be wary of lawyers who promise the moon or simply reflect back what you are saying. A good lawyer will calibrate your expectations to what you can realistically expect if you press forward. A good lawyer will tell you when your dispute is not worth pursuing.

5. When Don't You Need a Lawyer?

When you don't need a lawyer depends on many factors, but there are steps to evaluating whether or not you want to retain a lawyer and to what extent (e.g., just for a consult, just to help you draft part of the case, or full representation).

In Sample 2 I've developed a way to score your case to determine where it lies on the spectrum between really needing a lawyer and perhaps being okay representing yourself.

6. Lawyers and Misconduct

Lawyers have comprehensive rules that tell them how to professionally maintain certain standards of conduct. The rules range from a duty to be courteous to rules about who a lawyer can and cannot represent (if a lawyer represents a person with whom he or she has a "conflict," the lawyer can be professionally disciplined). These rules of professional conduct are set in each jurisdiction to which the lawyer is a member of the bar. (Lawyers belong to "the bar" in the province in which they were admitted. Lawyers can be admitted in more than one province.) Rules governing lawyers' conduct are typically available online. For example, in BC go to lawsociety.bc.ca.

If you believe that a lawyer has violated a rule of professional conduct, you can file a complaint with the disciplinary organization that regulates lawyer conduct in the jurisdiction where the lawyer is admitted. For example, in British Columbia a complaint would be made to the Law Society of BC. Complaints are taken very seriously and these organizations have the power to impose sanctions on a lawyer such as, in extreme cases, disbarring the lawyer. More typically a lawyer who has violated rules of professional conduct is issued a warning, or some sort of remedial sanction (to attend courses, for example), or pay a fine.

One thing a complaint about a lawyer cannot do is change the outcome of a judge's decision. While a lawyer's misconduct might be grounds for an appeal or a re-hearing, a complaint does not itself affect what happened in court. If you want to change a judge's decision, you should investigate your appeal options.

If you suspect lawyer misconduct, your first step might be to gather more information about whether there is in fact misconduct. If you think the misconduct had an effect on a judge's decision, you should try to speak to a different lawyer about your appeal options. Complaining about a lawyer will not itself change a judge's decision.

Sample 2
Do You Need a Lawyer?

1. **What court are you in?**

   If you are in Small Claims court, proceedings are generally designed to be more user-friendly for non-lawyers. Some other courts have relaxed rules that make the proceedings easier for non-represented persons. For example, in British Columbia, family court cases often can proceed in either Supreme Court or Provincial Court. Provincial Court tends to be less formal and thus easier for *pro se* litigants.

   Courts that are *pro se* friendly versus courts that are not *pro se* friendly

   Circle one (one indicating *pro se* friendly such as Small Claims Court, and five indicating not *pro se* friendly)

1	2	3	4	5

2. **How complicated is the case?**

   First, how many claims or issues are there? Is there one issue? For example, say you hired a contractor to paint your home. You paid him but he only completed half the job. Or are there many claims or issues? For example, say you are separating from your spouse and you disagree about parenting time, child support, alimony, and how to divide your assets.

   Second, how complicated is it to prove your case? Sometimes, all you need is one witness who will testify. Other times, you will need to sift through boxes of business records. Also, some cases require expert witnesses. For example, if you and your spouse own a business together and you disagree on what it is worth, you may need to retain a business evaluator/appraiser.

   The more straightforward the issues are and what you need to do to prove your case, the easier it will be for you to represent yourself. (Presumably your legal fees, if you did hire a lawyer, will be less too.)

   Circle one (one indicating not complicated versus five indicating very complicated)

1	2	3	4	5

3. **Is settlement likely?**

   If you and the other side are talking and close to making a deal, you may be able to get by without a lawyer. However, a lawyer may be helpful for the last stage; say you've reached an oral agreement and now you want to make sure it is put into a binding legal document, a settlement agreement. One cost-effective way to iron out any outstanding wrinkles and to get the agreement reduced to writing is to hire a mediator. In any event, being close to settlement is a good thing and will mean you are less likely to tie up resources in a legal struggle and legal fees.

Circle one (one indicating possible versus five indicating unlikely)

1 2 3 4 5

4. What resources are available to you?

Some areas of law have excellent and reliable web-based information from the Courts or legal aid organizations.

In British Columbia, www.clicklaw.bc.ca is operated by the Courthouse Libraries BC. It is a valuable resource. There is also www.justiceeducation.ca. For family law specific information, there is www.familylaw.lss.bc.ca, which is maintained by the Legal Services Society of BC (the organization that provides legal aid).

Circle one (one indicating good resources versus five indicating resources are few and far between)

1 2 3 4 5

5. Do you have time?

Representing yourself takes time. It's not just a matter of booking off a few days for the trial. Every case is going to require time to fill out court forms, arrange for service, talk to the other side about settlement, and time to organize your Trial Book. If you have witnesses (besides yourself) and documents, you will need to set time aside for interviewing witnesses and for organizing and then exchanging documents per discovery rules.

Circle one (one indicating you have tons of time versus five indicating you barely have time to read this)

1 2 3 4 5

6. What is at stake?

How important is the legal dispute? If it is about $500 and you spend that much on dinners out every month, well, it is probably not worth your while going to court anyway. However, if it is about having $500 a month paid for child support and this would really make a difference for your family, then the stakes are higher. The higher the stakes, the wiser you would be to get legal help.

Circle one (one indicating low stakes versus five high stakes)

1 2 3 4 5

Sample 2 — Continued

Add up all the numbers you circled to come up with your score_____

Let me begin by saying, if you can afford it, you're always going to be better off with a good lawyer in any legal dispute. A good lawyer will tell you what he or she can do to help and when he or she doesn't need to help. Having a good lawyer retained and reviewing at least what you're doing is not a bad idea in any circumstance.

Lawyer's fees can range from as low as $25 for a first meeting through a bar association referral (or free if you can talk to a lawyer for the day), all the way up to tens of thousands of dollars. I typically tell clients in family law proceedings to expect to pay around $10,000 per day of trial.

Fortunately, few cases actually go to trial. But before trial, settlement negotiations and prep generally cost at least $1,000 and up. If you are retaining a lawyer, he or she should give you a ballpark figure, given what might and might not happen in the buildup to trial.

That being said, take the scoring with a grain of salt. There is no exact science here and every case is different. The bottom line, really, will be what you can afford.

A score of 12 or lower indicates there you are probably in a good position to consider representing yourself. This may change as litigation heats up, but you're well positioned.

Ideally, of course, you'd have a lawyer but that option is one you may not be able to make and you're better off than most people at choosing to go it alone. Scores between 13 and 18 suggest that you really should consider having a lawyer but that the factors to successfully represent yourself are there, you're just going to have work extra hard.

If your score is higher than 19, I strongly recommend you consider trying to get legal representation, full if possible, but at least in some limited form.

5
Discovery: Sharing Evidence and Information

1. Discovery

Discovery is the mandatory process where you and the other side share all information in your possession that is relevant to any claim or defence in the case. It's where you get to discover what evidence the other side has before trial.

2. What Is Evidence?

Evidence is the factual information that you use to prove or disprove your case. Here are some examples of evidence:

- Testimony of a witness.

- Documents such as a tax return, receipt, letter, or bill.

- Physical objects. For example, a key used to damage your car or, of course, a knife in a murder prosecution.

Evidence law is the set of rules that govern what evidence can be used by the judge or jury in your case. Not all evidence is allowed to be used at trial. A judge is bound by rules of evidence and will decide what evidence he or she (and the jury if there is one) can use to make the decision. This is known as admissible evidence; evidence that court rules and the law in your jurisdiction deem reliable. Inadmissible evidence may not be used by the judge (or jury) to make a decision. Inadmissible evidence is deemed to be unreliable.

Admissible evidence may be:

- Firsthand knowledge of a relevant event such as seeing an accident, observing a parent's care of children, observing damage to a vehicle, etc.

- An original document that is relevant to a proceeding such as a photograph, a contract, or a receipt.

Admissible evidence is generally not:

- Secondhand information. For example, describing a conversation you overheard in which a person describes a car accident. This is known as hearsay. (Hearsay may be admissible in certain circumstances; see section 2.2).

- A witness' opinion of an issue at trial. For example, if your witness says that the other side is a bad parent, that is an opinion. It would be more helpful if that witness instead offered examples she or he has witnessed of bad parenting by the other side. (e.g., he or she observed the children returning from parenting time hungry and in unwashed clothes). However, if the witness is found by the court to be an expert on a subject (e.g., a doctor who is qualified to identify injuries related to domestic violence or an appraiser who is qualified to value a business), the expert's opinion may be admissible.

- What you think should happen. The claims and relief you have requested from the court are not evidence.

- What you or a witness thinks happened; a guess or a theory is not evidence of something actually happening. You can offer a guess or a theory during argument at the close of your case.

The rules of evidence are complicated and vary between jurisdictions and areas of law. This book is meant to provide a rough overview of the law of evidence only. To prepare for your hearing you should:

1. Understand the elements that you need to prove or disprove to win your case in your jurisdiction and for your kind of case.

2. Gather information that proves or disproves the elements of your claims, the claims of the other side, and any defences.

3. Determine whether that information is admissible or not in your trial.

2.1 Determining admissibility: Learning the law

So, how do you figure out the rules for evidence in your jurisdiction? Your first resource should be the Rules of Court. Though evidence law can be tricky, the fact of the matter is that in most basic civil trials (small business disputes, family law, housing, and debt cases) evidence law runs on a few basic principles. The information presented should be fair and reliable. For example, if a witness says that you never paid the money you allege you did, well, it wouldn't be fair if that witness is the other party's boyfriend and is just guessing, would it? So, a court should rule that that witness' evidence is inadmissible in this regard.

So what is admissible evidence? Here are some broad-stroke considerations:

1. Firsthand knowledge: During the testimony of a witness, you will want him or her to stick to the facts of which he or she has firsthand knowledge.

2. Keep it relevant: Let's say the defendant lost custody of his children from a prior marriage ten years ago. Is this relevant to a hearing today about custody of the children from a new relationship? Yes; that information might be relevant to his ability to parent in the children's best interests.

   What about testimony about the fact that he took expensive ski trips during that relationship from ten years ago? Is that relevant to the issue of parenting time today? Probably not, but it may be relevant to the issue of alimony, if that is an issue. Relevance is a broad and elastic concept. Information that is relevant to a witness' credibility (whether he or she is believable) may have nothing to do with any of the claims in the case, but it is still relevant. The question of relevance is always up to the judge to decide. One thing to bear in mind is that generally you do not want to bore the Court with information of slight relevance. Stick to the evidence that truly moves your case forward so that your case makes an impact on the Court.

3. Stay away from confidential or privileged information: Settlement talks and letters are not admissible. Generally, you can't testify that the defendant offered you $2,000 to settle the case so he really does owe you money; those talks are confidential.

2.2 What is hearsay, and is it always bad?

Hearsay is a statement made outside of court by a non-witness that a witness repeats as testimony and is made to prove the truth of what it is about. Confusing? Let's take that a little slower.

Hearsay is:

1. A statement: Something someone said.

2. Spoken outside of court: That is, something someone said, say, last week walking down the street.

3. That a witness repeats: The person testifying is quoting what someone else said.

4. As testimony: In other words, on the witness stand (or maybe in a sworn affidavit).

5. Is made to prove the truth of what it is about: In other words, the reason for this testimony is to prove that what the statement is about is true. So, if I overheard John say that the truck was blue and then I testify in court that John said the truck was blue, what I'm trying to prove is that the truck is blue.

If a witness were to testify, "Allan said that John hit the child," this is a statement that someone other than the witness made and the reason it is part of the trial is to prove that the plaintiff actually did hit the child. Instead of using this hearsay statement, the party who wants to know whether Allan himself observed the plaintiff hitting the child should call Allan as a witness.

Hearsay is, generally, seen as unreliable and is not allowed. However, in Canada, rules of evidence may allow hearsay into evidence if it falls into one of several exceptions to hearsay. These exceptions include where its admission is necessary to prove a fact in issue and the evidence is reliable and where its helpfulness outweighs any prejudice it may cause. I know that sounds confusing; however, it may be helpful to simply ask yourself, "Is it fair that this statement be used by the judge?" The reason hearsay is often unfair is that if the statement relied upon the Court making a decision, the other side would not have had an opportunity to ask the speaker of the statement questions about it. For example, let's say that plaintiff Lucy Luck testified in court that her friend Armand Armani told her that he saw the defendant's car go through a red light and hit the plaintiff's bicycle. Now, the defendant will not be able to ask Lucy Luck questions about Armand Armani such as, "Where were you standing?" "Did you have a good view of the lights?" and "Did you observe if the bicyclist had a green light?" In other words, because the information is secondhand and Armand Armani is not present in court, the defendant doesn't have an opportunity to really test the testimony properly. Thus it probably isn't fair to allow this hearsay evidence. However, if Mr. Armani made this statement right after the accident (which means his memory was fresh) and then he himself died, then there might be more fairness in allowing this hearsay statement into evidence.

Sometimes Court Rules allow certain types of hearsay; for example, in BC civil courts, hearsay is allowed on interim (i.e., temporary) court applications as long as the source of the information is identified.

2.3 Weight: Not all evidence is created equal

The judge (or jury) will decide the weight (importance) of a piece of evidence. Just because evidence has been admitted into court, it does not mean that it will be given the same weight as other evidence or even any weight at all. For example, testimony about a material fact that is given in a believable manner and is not contradicted would be given more weight than testimony that is not believable and is contradicted by other evidence.

3. What Evidence Gets Shared in Discovery and How?

Remember the television moment when suddenly a new piece of evidence is produced in the middle of a trial? Well, that is not supposed to happen in a real trial. In fact, a judge will not allow a party to surprise the other side with evidence they haven't seen unless there is a very good reason why that evidence could not have been shared beforehand.

Due process rules generally require each side in a court case to disclose to the other side information that will help to prove or disprove a material fact in the case. (This happens either automatically or by request depending upon the relevant Court Rules.) This does mean you may have to disclose information that hurts, rather than helps, your case. Failure to do so can have severe consequences.

Discovery is the way you discover what the other side's case is about and they discover what your case is about. Once discovery is complete, you should have all the same information as the other side, and thus you should be able to evaluate the strengths and weaknesses of the other side's case, and they will be able to do the same.

Discovery can be time-consuming and tedious, both when providing discovery and obtaining information from the other side. Though pouring through the other side's documents does not usually result in a game-changing piece of information it is an essential step in preparing for trial. For example, I've spent days poring over financial statements in divorces hoping to find evidence that the opposing party is living a lifestyle that exceeds his or her income thus indicating that he or she is somehow receiving additional income (so called "cash jobs") on the side. I have yet to discover conclusive proof in a case that this is happening. Nonetheless, I will continue to read credit card and bank statements to make sure all the numbers add up. Information obtained in discovery provides building blocks for a successful trial.

I hate to say it, but in complex litigation, it can be very difficult for a self-represented person without legal training to understand the intricate rules and case law that apply to discovery. Indeed, a UK case on discovery and a lawyer's duty in that regard stated "A client left to himself could not know what is relevant, nor is he likely to realize that it is his obligation to disclose every relevant document, even a document which would establish, or go far to establish, against him his opponent's case." *Myers v. Elman*, [1940] A.C. 283 (H.L.). Granted, this case is dated and strides have been made in many courts to help *pro se* litigants navigate discovery. However, if the court you are in is not as progressive as some (e.g., most small claims courts have simplified discovery procedures), you should consult with a lawyer before disclosing documents that you are uncertain about or if the discovery you have received is not what you expected.

3.1 Documents and other physical information that should be disclosed: Yours and theirs

The scope for discovery is generally broad. This means that the net of what you need to disclose is cast wide and almost anything that could be relevant to a claim is shared. The following is a summary of the general procedure and tools for discovery.

The consequences for not disclosing relevant information can range from being prevented from using that evidence at trial to financial penalties being made against you.

What exactly are the things that are discoverable? Check your local Court Rules carefully. In BC, Supreme Court Civil Rule 7-1 covers the discovery of documents for certain civil matters before the Supreme Court. "Document" is defined in SCCR 1-1(1) as having an "extended meaning" which "includes a photograph, film, recording of sound, any record of a permanent or semi-permanent character, and any information recorded or stored by means of any device." Basically, any information that is reduced to writing, printing, or electronic file is a document. Photographs, receipts, bank statements, government records, business records, if relevant to the dispute or the amount of damages sought, are generally discoverable. This doesn't mean that they will necessarily be admissible at trial. The scope for discovery is wider than what is admissible at trial. In other words, discovery will probably produce more material for you and the other side to review than what a judge will allow himself or herself (or a jury) to review and thus choose to rely or not rely on.

3.2 Information that should generally not be disclosed: Privileged, confidential, or irrelevant

There are exceptions to what you have to share in discovery. Check your local rules; however, the following generally do not have to be disclosed:

1. **Trial preparation materials:** Generally, material that is prepared in anticipation of a trial is not discoverable. (There are exceptions to this rule.) Historically, this rule applies to lawyers and protects the work they generate in preparation for trial such as notes of their mental impressions, expert opinions they obtain, and their legal research. The rule also applies to a person who is self-represented.

   For example, let's say that you are in a dispute about the purchase of a used car. You claim that the timing belt was not replaced as required by contract prior to the purchase. You decide to hire a mechanic to provide a written, expert opinion on the timing belt. Your communications and that mechanic's written opinion may not have to be disclosed. Other examples would include drafts of letters you've written and your notes.

2. **Solicitor-client privilege:** To allow lawyers and their clients to be able to have frank, honest communication, communications between a lawyer and his or her client are generally not something the other side can obtain. (There are some jurisdictions and courts that have a narrower definition, so check

your jurisdiction's rules carefully.) That means these communications do not have to be disclosed if requested by the other side, but doesn't mean you are prevented from disclosing this kind of information if you want to. Because you and your lawyer hold this right, you can choose to disclose the information. However, once you open this door, a court might consider that you have waived more than you bargained for and allow more to be disclosed than you originally intended. (In other words, if you decide to disclose privileged information to another person, the material will no longer be solicitor-client privileged and a court might decide that you have waived this privilege with respect to other information too.)

Generally, this privilege applies to those conversations or letters you may have with a lawyer in which he or she provides you with a legal opinion. There are exceptions to this rule in most jurisdictions. For example, if a third party was present during the communication, that person is not covered by the privilege and thus could be made to testify. This may also be considered a waiver of the privilege. As well, if you tell your lawyer that you are going to commit a crime (not that you committed a serious crime in the past; a lawyer should not disclose that without your permission), a lawyer generally has a duty to report that.

3. **Irrelevant information:** You do not have to disclose something that is totally irrelevant. Check your local rules carefully in cases where that information might help someone to find relevant information.

4. How Do You Do Discovery?

Discovery generally occurs after the plaintiff has filed and served her case and the defendant has also filed and served the defence, and any claims. Depending on your jurisdiction, discovery either begins when you receive a request for discovery from the other side, or automatically according to timelines in your jurisdiction's Court Rules.

Generally, exchanging documents is the first step in discovery before other discovery tools such as an oral examination for discovery. This is because the information you glean from document discovery and other forms of written discovery such as interrogatories (written questions) can help you to ask the right questions at an examination for discovery.

4.1 When you have information to be disclosed

4.1a Automatic duty

If you have a document or other information that is relevant to the case, check your Court Rules to see if you have to disclose it automatically. In civil matters in the BC Supreme Court, for example, a litigant is required to prepare and serve on the other side within a set time period a list of documents "that are or have been in the party's possession or control and that could, if available, be used by any party of record at trial to prove or disprove a material fact," as well as "all other documents to which the party intends to refer at trial." (BC Supreme Court Civil Rule 7-1.) Each party must allow the other side to look at the documents listed and copy them. Court Rules require the list to adhere to a certain format.

What if you've already exchanged documents and then something new turns up? The duty to disclose is usually ongoing, so, yes you should disclose any newly received information that is disclosable.

4.1b Duty upon request

You may receive a letter requesting disclosure from the other side. For example, you may receive a letter listing certain kinds of information. Generally, as long as the information does not fall within an exception (see below) and is relevant, you should disclose it. Legal battles about what should and should not be disclosed have left a complicated trail of case law; research this area carefully for your jurisdiction. However, if you do not disclose a relevant document, the other side may file a Motion for Discovery to ask the Court to order you to disclose information. Unless there is a good reason not to disclose information (e.g., it is not relevant to the case, it is legally privileged, or it is not in your possession or control), there is little advantage in opposing such a motion. In fact, opposing it without a good reason may result in court costs against you (you'll have to pay the other side). Remember, you have to disclose both information that helps and information that hurts your case. If you are unsure, talk to a lawyer.

Be mindful of any deadlines to provide the information. Also, read the requests and your Court Rules carefully to determine if you just have to make the information available, or if you have to provide copies, who has to pay for those. You and the other side will have to come to some agreements with respect to exchanging documents. I recommend making this process as easy for the other side as possible so that they do the same for you. In my experience, judges frown on unnecessary roadblocks to the flow of information between parties.

4.2 Information the other side holds

It is critical that you obtain and look at all information relevant to the claims you are making or are being made against you.

If you have not received disclosure from the other side, you should first ascertain if there is any automatic requirement that it be provided (if there is, you'll have to disclose your relevant information too — see above). For example, in BC civil matters you should generally receive a list of the other side's documents. Typically, in BC a lawyer will write to the disclosing attorney and request copies of the documents that the lawyer wishes to see. A disclosing law firm will then bill the requesting lawyer for the copying. As an unrepresented party, you can certainly ask a law firm to do this. However, there is no requirement that the law firm actually make photocopies. In fact, all they have to do is to make the documents available to you for inspection and copying. Unless you bring your own photocopier to the law firm, they will likely charge you for each copy. Find out ahead of time what they will charge and if they will instead provide you with electronic copies free of charge, which you can print. If there is an automatic disclosure requirement and the deadline has passed, but you have not received any disclosure, you should write a letter to the other side reminding them of the disclosure requirement and informing them that you will have to go to court if they do not provide the information.

If there is no automatic disclosure requirement for your jurisdiction and your kind of case, you should find out what your Court Rules require for you to serve a request for disclosure on the other side. There may be a specific form or wording you will have to use.

Often, when I receive disclosure from the other side, I find that there are things missing. For example, maybe they've provided bank statements for the past two years when they were supposed to provide statements for the last three. Or, they haven't provided photographs I know they took and are on their computer. In those cases, I write to the other side and specifically list the documents I am requesting with as much detail as possible. I word this letter politely but firmly. If the documents are not forthcoming, this letter may need to be shown to the court (attached to an affidavit describing my efforts to obtain disclosure) so I want it to make me look good.

Generally, the documents disclosed should be kept confidential. You can usually show them to a potential witness or an expert for purposes of preparing for trial.

4.3 Documents in the possession of a non-party: Third-party documents

It is usually possible to obtain relevant information from persons or entities that are not parties to the court case. Procedures to do so vary. A first step is to write to the third party and request a copy of the document. If that is not successful, in BC, you may make a chambers application to ask the court to issue an order requiring disclosure of the document [SCCR 7-1(18)]. Check your Court Rules and law library to learn the legal requirements and how to do this.

4.4 Asking questions: Oral and written discovery

4.4a Oral questions

There are several different ways to ask questions of the opposing party or witnesses that may lead to helpful evidence. Sometimes the people you are asking questions of are required to answer, even if the information is harmful to their case.

By all means phone people who might have useful information about your claim. Ask them politely if they are willing to talk to you, but they do not have to. It is an old truism of law that there is no property in a witness. That means that no one owns a witness and whether they are going to testify for you or against you; you can contact them and, if they are willing, talk to them. Take notes of those conversations. (Generally, your notes will not be admissible as evidence.) If the information is helpful, you might consider using their information at trial by calling them as witnesses.

Can you use the phone call or interview at trial? No, although there are always exceptions. You will need to ask that person to be a witness (see Chapter 9 on how to do that) and hope that his or her testimony in court is the same as what you previously heard. If the person's testimony at trial is different from what she told you on the phone, you can ask her why her statement is inconsistent.

While lawyers are not allowed to directly contact another party who is represented (they have to contact the party's lawyer), a party certainly can contact another party directly. (This is one advantage a self-represented person has over a lawyer!) The other party may not wish to talk to you and has no duty to do so. There are, however, ways to require them to talk to you so read on.

4.4b Interogatories

Interrogatories are questions put in writing to another party (not a witness) which they are required to answer in writing. Interrogatories can be used during a trial because they are sworn evidence like an affidavit. Sometimes you need the Court's permission or the other party's consent to ask interrogatories. (Unfortunately this is the case in British Columbia.) Often, the Court or Court Rules will limit the number of questions you can ask.

The party served with interrogatories must respond within a certain amount of time. He or she can object to particular questions based on the rules of evidence, for example, if the question asks something that is not within the party's knowledge or requires an expert opinion such as a medical question or simply is not relevant. Responses are generally sworn testimony (in BC by affidavit, signed in front of a notary).

Be careful answering interrogatories. Usually, lawyers help their clients provide an honest but carefully worded answer. This is so that a client's answer does not inadvertently admit some element of the claim against them that they do not intend or make them appear not credible. Remember that you are answering under oath and if the other side later is able to persuade a judge that you were not honest, your credibility on anything else in the case will come into question. In other words, if you mistakenly say that the car that hit you was grey in your interrogatory answers but later, at trial, testify that it was red, the lawyer on the other side will be quick to tell the judge (and jury) that your testimony is unreliable.

There are several reasons why interrogatories are useful:

1. They are a good way to establish facts that both sides agree on so that the trial is not bogged down. For example, in a personal injury lawsuit both sides might agree that the accident occurred at Main and 100th Street, that the traffic lights were not functioning, and that the defendant was driving a black Lexus and the plaintiff a Ford pickup.

2. To prepare for an examination for discovery or a trial, interrogatories may be a useful way to obtain the facts as the other side understands them. Because the answers are in writing and sworn, they can be used later when cross-examining a party if their answers on the witness stand differ from their interrogatories.

3. They are relatively inexpensive compared with the costs of an examination for discovery.

The disadvantage of interrogatories is that the other side has the time to carefully construct an answer. Sometimes it is better to get a quicker (and less managed) answer at an examination for discovery. In family law cases, I rarely use interrogatories because the answers, which read as if a lawyer has sifted over every word, serve the other side's interests. It is much better to surprise the other side at a deposition or at trial with my questions, as long as I know the answers ahead of time.

There is generally a continuing obligation to update your answers to interrogatory answers. For example, if you were asked whether you are employed and answered, "No," but later become employed, you should consider amending or refiling your answer.

4.4c Examinations for Discovery

Ah, the power of an examination for discovery. You, the plaintiff or defendant, can compel the other side (or a witness) to attend a meeting where he or she must answer all questions you properly put to him or her.

The first one I sat in on was when I was an intern at a law firm. The lawyer I was working for had brought a party all the way from Germany. Frankly, we thought he wouldn't show but he called our bluff. After all, usually the party holding the examination for discovery must pay the travel costs of the person submitting to it. The lawyer got worked up and aggressive, the defendant's lawyer objected to questions, there was a heated private session between lawyers, and then the questioning continued. The defendant, dressed in a linen jacket, looking rested and relaxed, answered each question simply. He did not appear fazed; he looked distracted, sometimes annoyed. He was enduring a petty bureaucrat's moment of glory.

What was it worth? Well, to my mind, no. No new information of significance came to light. Yes, we got to see what the defendant was like under pressure and at trial that knowledge would have helped us. But was it worth the cost of flying the witness all the way from Germany? Probably not.

There is no judge sitting in on an examination for discovery. It is very expensive to have the transcript typed, and that transcript may never actually be shown to the judge or jury at trial, let alone make a difference at that trial. For most of the litigation I've been involved with, it is rarely worth the expense. However, for high stakes or complicated cases, an examination for discovery may be a powerful tool, perhaps up there in the top three strategic tools you have at your disposal. Knowing whether or not to use an examination for discovery is a difficult strategic decision even for a seasoned lawyer.

In any case, it is always important to go through the pros and cons of examining the opposing party or a witness. Sometimes it can push a party towards settlement or be an important step in winning your case. Sometimes it is simply a waste of valuable resources.

So, what is an examination for discovery? It is an opportunity for one party to cross-examine another party under oath. (You may be able to examine a third party too, but in BC, for example, there must be some issue between you and that witness.) Depending on your jurisdiction and the type of proceeding, you may be required to ask for permission from the Court (this is know as "leave") by making a motion to hold an examination for discovery.

Like interrogatories, an examination of the other side is a useful way to gain understanding of the other side's case. It is also a useful tool for settlement because:

1. It tends to signal to the other side that you are serious about taking the matter to trial. This is because it will require you to invest money in the case to pay for expenses such as the stenographer, room, transcripts, and witness fees.

2. Meeting face to face often helps with settlement negotiations. The party being examined may be more willing to shift his or her position rather than face cross-examination.

3. For the examiner (i.e., the person asking questions and who has requested the examination for discovery), learning about the strength of the other side's case may shift his or her position and thus make the party more open to negotiation.

The big downside to an examination for discovery is cost. It isn't cheap. The biggest expense will be for the stenographer and the transcript.

Because it must be recorded, arrangements for a room and a stenographer (someone who types what is being said) must be made. You will have to contact an agency that does this work. Generally, the parties agree on a mutually convenient date and place such as the stenographer's office or the office of a lawyer, not the courthouse.

Generally, you should wait until all the pleadings have been filed (the claims, defences, and counterclaims) so that it is clear what all the issues are. It is also helpful to schedule the examination after you have completed discovery of documents and any interrogatories. That is because you will want to use those documents and interrogatories to ask the person you are examining questions. If the other side won't agree on a mutually convenient time, then you may have to go ahead and send them notice of a time you think is best. They will have to attend (or go to court to ask the Court to change the time). You will have to pay the stenographer for his or her time and use of the room. If you are unable to pay (indigent), you may be able to ask the Court for payment or for the other side to pay.

Notice of the examination must be properly served on the person being examined. The person who asks the questions must do this. You may also be required, depending on your jurisdiction, to send travel expenses and a witness fee. Your Court Rules will say how much notice the other side must be given. Generally, the notice must be in a format and with wording that is required by your Court Rules. Usually, you can also tell the person to be examined to bring specified documents with him or her to the examination for inspection. Though an examination for discovery may be a tool to obtain documents, ideally you will have obtained all documents previously via request for production of documents.

4.4ci What happens in an examination for discovery?

After checking in, you will be shown to a room where the examination takes place. Generally, the parties and their lawyers are present. The judge will not be there, nor will a judge later read and admit into evidence the entire transcript unless it has been introduced at trial.

A stenographer or other person who can record the examination will be present. Often, that person will administer the oath to tell the truth.

The stenographer will have no power to make any decision. He or she is not "in charge" and you should not expect him or her to explain the law to you or explain how things should happen.

The stenographer will generally want to take a break in the morning, at lunch, and mid-afternoon. An examination for discovery is often booked for at least a day. If you have only a few very specific questions, you can book it for a half day. If you and the other side get into a heated argument and the stenographer begins to think a party is losing control of himself or herself, the stenographer may give you a warning that the meeting will end if the behaviour continues. Usually, once the stenographer has indicated readiness, the examining party will identify himself or herself for the record and ask the other party for their name and address, as well as the name of any lawyers present. Some jurisdictions may limit the length of an examination for discovery. In BC, for example, examinations must not exceed seven hours without permission of the Court.

Not everything has to be "on the record." There will be portions of the examination that you do not want the stenographer to put in the transcript. For example, "Should we order in lunch now?" or "May I have a bathroom break?" As well, examinations for discovery will lead to issues that need discussion such as whether a certain question is appropriate, settlement discussions, and discussions about tone and manner.

A lawyer or a party might bang the table, stand up, swear, or walk out. This kind of behaviour is not appropriate. (If it continues, it might be worthwhile to consider whether to end the meeting; however, that is risky as a hearing may ensue about whether the examination for discovery should continue and court costs could be allocated if a party is found to have improperly ended a deposition.) In any of these circumstances, you can ask the lawyer or party on the other side to go "off the record." If they agree, confirm with the stenographer that you are off the record so that the following conversation will not be typed and should not form part of the transcript. To restart the examination, let the stenographer know that your are going back on the record.

The examination is in the form of cross-examination. That means that you can ask leading questions. "You killed the maid, didn't you?" or "You have a bank account in the Caymans, don't you?" Leading questions are questions that can be answered with "Yes" or "No." See Chapter 9 on how to form these kind of questions. As well, you can and should also use open-ended questions at the examination. This is because your goal is to gather information and, at this stage of the litigation, you probably don't fully understand or know what the other side's story is. You might not like what they say, but remember that every word the other party is saying is something that you will have a chance to address at trial, and you need to know the bad as well as the good.

So, keep asking those hard questions that elicit testimony that isn't good for you. Get it all out so you know what you're up against and so that the other side can't change his or her story later.

Also, it's a good idea to ask questions like, "Is there anything else you recall?" before moving on to a new area of questioning. If the witness refers to a document you haven't seen before, ask him or her to produce it; if it's not there, ask for it to be produced after the meeting (and follow up so he or she does).

4.4cii How to answer when you are asked questions

Some tips for answering questions:

- Wait for the question to be fully stated. Listen to it carefully.

- Only answer the question asked. Do not offer longwinded explanations or information that was not asked for. (Be patient, the time to offer your story the way you want to will come.)

- If you do not understand the question, ask the examiner to restate it. (Confusing, ambiguous questions are common.) Don't guess at the question.

- If the examiner starts talking about a document and asking you questions about it, ask to see it. It's better to have it in front of you rather than guess about what it contains.

- Be honest.

- Relax. Do what you need to stay calm. Take a breath, ask for a break, picture the lawyer examining you in a funny costume.

- Don't argue with the examiner. If he or she is being hostile and badgering you, ask to take a break, go off the record and ask him or her to be more civil.

- If you don't know the answer to the question, it's okay to say "I don't know." However, there is a fine line between answering "I don't know" and circumstances where you can say "I'm not sure and I can find out." You should answer "I don't know" to a question about something you never knew the answer to and never will. If the question is about something you could figure out, and in fact you probably will have an answer when it comes to the trial, it should be answered by stating that you do not recall but you can find out (e.g., if you were asked where you were living in 20XX and answered, "I don't know," that sounds evasive). These are often questions about location, time, and distance. Court Rules in BC, for instance, require people being examined to inform themselves not only as to what is within their knowledge (e.g., reading over a calendar to remember the dates), but also matters that they can find out about. If the person being examined doesn't know the answer, but has a way of finding out, he or she may be asked to respond to the question by letter later after finding out the answer. This is fairly common in examinations for discovery. The questions and answers in that responding letter are deemed to still be under oath [in BC, see SCCR 7-2(24)].

- Do not answer with head nods or other confusing sounds (e.g., "mm-hmm"). Answer "Yes" or "No."

4.4ciii Objections

There are two main areas that are off-limits at an examination for discovery:

- Irrelevant questions. Remember that the scope for examination is broad and that an improper question should clearly be seeking information that is unrelated to the matters at issue.

- Questions about privileged information. For example, conversations with a lawyer where you are seeking legal advice.

If you are being examined and an objectionable question is asked, you can state that you object to the question. You might go off the record to discuss with the examiner whether or not you are correct. Generally, you should answer the question despite your objection if the only basis of your objection is irrelevancy, and the other side is able to draw some link however tenuous between the question and the issues in the case. However, privileged information should not be supplied.

You can also object on the ground that the question has asked for information that is not admissible per your jurisdiction's evidence laws. Some of these grounds for objection are discussed in Chapter 9. Because a judge is not present, it is generally advisable to say you object but answer the question nevertheless because, after all, the judge is not present and you will have a chance to persuade him or her about the admissibility of your answer to that question at trial if the other side seeks to ask the question again or to introduce this part of the transcript.

If the examiner feels that an objection and refusal to answer is wrong, he or she can file a motion to ask the Court to decide if the person being examined should answer it or not. If the Court does decide that the question should be answered it will generally be at another examination for discovery.

4.4civ Documents are exhibits

There may be times where the examiner will want to show a document to a witness. For example, to ask if it is his or her signature on a contract or if he or she recognizes a cheque. To keep order in the examination and to clearly identify which document is being introduced, any document referred to should be described on the record and then given an exhibit number. Usually, the stenographer will organize and number each exhibit and keep a list of all exhibits (e.g., contract between March Hare and Queen of Hearts, dated March 21, 20XX, Exhibit 1). This does not mean that the document will be determined by a judge as admissible, necessarily. The exhibit numbers at trial never are the same as the exhibit numbers from examination. While the stenographer is busy marking an exhibit (usually, he or she will put a sticker on it with the exhibit number), be sure not to continue the examination questioning.

4.4cv What is the role of the lawyer in the examination for discovery?

If a lawyer is conducting an examination for discovery, his or her role is to ask questions of the witness, not to provide legal advice. He or she is not in charge of when breaks may be taken; that is by agreement. However, the lawyer is in charge of the flow of the examination; he or she gets to choose the questions and how they are delivered.

If a lawyer is attending with the person being examined, he or she is there primarily to object to improper questions and keep the examination moving forward in a fair manner for his or her client. If he or she answers questions, those answers are not evidence and not under oath. It is important that only the witness answer the questions. A lawyer can be helpful in finding documents for his or her client and can also seek to clarify a witness' answer. That might be helpful but, again, it is not evidence. Much of a lawyer's work is done before the examination by prepping the client for the kinds of questions that might be asked and offering guidance for providing appropriate answers.

4.4cvi Re-examination and the transcript

It's almost over! If you are being examined, you may when the other side is finished asking questions, depending on your jurisdiction, have the right for "re-examination." This means that if you had a lawyer, he or she could ask you questions which might be helpful in clarifying something that was ambiguous in your testimony.

You may feel very tempted after being examined for several hours to take this opportunity to "set the record straight." In my experience, this is not a good idea. You will probably be exhausted and reeling from the examination. If you really need to say something, grit your teeth for now and put it in a letter later. If you can consult with a lawyer, do so. Re-examination is not usually necessary because there is no judge at the examination to whom you can prove your point.

At the end of the examination, you should ask the stenographer for an opportunity to review the transcript before it is finalized. The stenographer will send it to you once it is typed up. Read it over carefully to make sure it accurately records the questions asked and your responses. This is not an opportunity, however, to change a bad answer.

Examining a Company?

What if you are suing a company? Who can you examine? That is a strategic question. It will be important to examine a person who has authority to speak on behalf of the entity being sued. You don't want to go to the expense of subpoenaing an employee who has no knowledge of the case.

⚜ ⚜ ⚜

5. Preparation for an Examination for Discovery

If you are the examiner personally asking the questions, you should read over the pleadings very carefully. Then read any affidavits the witness may have sworn. Write out questions ahead of time.

Organize documents you want to show to the witness and ask questions about. Have three copies ready of each: one for the witness, one for you, and one for the stenographer to mark as an exhibit.

Read through Chapter 9: Witnesses, which describes how to cross-examine a witness. An examination for discovery is not the best place to catch a witness in a lie or impeach him or her. (See Chapter 9 for further discussion of impeachment.) If that happens, great, but, strategically, you may prefer that to happen at trial. Remember that no judge is present at this time, so you cannot "win" an examination. Your game plan, in addition to increasing settlement opportunities, is to learn more about the strengths and weakness of the other side's case. Information is what you are seeking and the scope is broad. You can ask questions about the witness' background ("Do you have any criminal convictions?"), employment, and ability to observe and remember details. This could range from the witness' disabilities (does the person wear contacts and was the person wearing them on the day he or she observed something important?) to the weather on the day the person observed something important.

I recommend that you practice asking your questions ahead of time. You may want to ask a friend to role-play and pretend to be the witness.

If you are being examined, your goal is to be as relaxed and comfortable as possible so that you can understand the questions and answer them with as little stress and emotion as possible. This is so that your answers are accurate and don't provide too little or too much information. Imagine that a judge is listening in; you will want to sound frank and honest. Not evasive, not upset, and not as if you're trying to over-explain anything.

It is also helpful for the examinee to role play. This isn't to practice a canned answer so much as to focus on listening to the question and answering only that question. You should not offer long-winded explanations but focus on answering the question in as few words as possible. Make those words count: Clear and accurate to the best of your knowledge.

Also, you will want to gauge how tired you are becoming as you are being questioned. Listen to your body's cues for when your concentration is weakening or you are becoming triggered by the other side and know when to ask for a break.

You will also find role playing helpful in testing the limits of your knowledge. If you do not know the answer to a question, don't ever guess. Tell the examiner you don't know. Even if you have a guess that you think is really good, it doesn't matter. You are under oath and you wouldn't want to swear to something unless you are sure that it is correct.

6. Requests for Admission

Requests for admission are a useful way to narrow issues so that matters that are not in dispute do not become an unnecessary distraction or confuse the court. Anything that is admitted as true will be taken as proven in court. Basically, you send (per your jurisdiction's rules of court) to the other party a notice in writing that requests the other party either admit or deny the truth of a fact you allege. Requests for Admission can also be used to admit to the authenticity of a document. For example, by asking if the attached document contains the party's signature.

Typically, the party served with a Request for Admission must respond within a certain time period. If that party fails to respond as required (which is always in writing), within the time period, that party is deemed to have admitted to the truth of the fact. Therefore, if you receive a Request for Admission, immediately put the deadline for a response in your calendar!

The value of Requests for Admission is that any fact that is admitted is admissible at trial as if it had been proven.

Here are a few examples (note that the wording may be different in your jurisdiction and you should obtain an example):

1. If you are in a dispute about ownership of certain business assets, and it is not clear what the other side's position is on some: "Is it not true that you hold legal title to a Ford F-150 with BC licence plate number XXXX?"

2. If you are in a dispute about a contract, "Admit that the following document is signed by you on page 4; a written document dated September 7, 20XX, and bearing the signature of John Johnsby on page 4."

3. If you are in a dispute about parenting time in which you allege the other side misses scheduled parenting time, "Admit that on July 5, 20XX, you did not spend any parenting time with the children."

A request for admission must be carefully drafted. Read relevant Court Rules carefully. It is important to break down each fact into a separate request.

For example, take the following statement: "Admit that on April 15, 20XX, the Defendant John Doe mopped the floor of the business but did not place a sign warning customers that the floor was wet." There are two facts alleged: That the floor was mopped on April 15, 20XX, and that a warning sign was not placed. It would be better to break this down into two factual statements and thus two requests for admission. You may list in numbered paragraphs separate requests.

Make sure you stick to the facts. Simplicity is always best; do not add inflammatory language or exaggeration. Look over the reasons the other party can object to your request and make sure you do not draft a request to which he or she can object.

6.1 Answering requests for admission

What should you say when answering requests for admission? Depending on your jurisdiction, your choices are usually one of the following:

1. Admit the truth of the fact. For example, if the request states that you mopped the floor of your business on April 15, 20XX, your response would be to admit that this was true. Make sure you are admitting to everything that is asserted. If the request contains some information that is true but some that is not, you can admit in part and deny in part (or you can object to the question. See #3 below). For example, if the request states that you mopped the floor of your business on April 15, 20XX, but did not place a sign warning customers that the floor was wet, you could admit that you mopped the floor but deny that you did not place a warning sign.

2. Specifically deny the truth of the fact. For example, if the request states that you signed a contract but in fact you did not, you would state that you deny signing the contract. If part of the request is true, you should admit that part but deny the part that is not true.

3. Object to the request for admission if it is inappropriate and objectionable on some ground of evidence law. If you object, you must specifically state that you refuse to admit the truth of the fact on grounds such as:

   - **Privilege:** Explain the privilege. For example, if the request is to admit that your lawyer advised you that you had a losing case.

   - **Irrelevance:** Explain why the fact is irrelevant.

   - **The request is improper:** Explain why the request is improper. For example, it may be vague or contain multiple compounded facts.

4. Explain that you don't know. You should take reasonable steps to ascertain whether a statement is true or not by reviewing your records. However, if the question is beyond the scope of

your knowledge, explain that you cannot truthfully admit or deny the request because you do not have knowledge of the matter even though you have consulted the records and information available to you.

7. What to Do When the Other Side Isn't Complying with Discovery Rules

All too often, a court case turns into a paper chase. Let's say you send a list of interrogatories to the other side, and the response comes a week late and half the questions are not answered. Or, there's an automatic disclosure rule and you end up with only, you believe, half of what the other side should have sent you. What should you consider doing?

1. Start with a letter with a deadline: Let the other side know of the deficiency, what the deadline was, and that they've missed it. Tell them what can happen when someone doesn't comply with discovery rules. Then, give them an opportunity to supply the missing information. Often, I give a couple of weeks. I tell them that I may have to go to court to ask the court to enforce the discovery rules if they do not comply and that they may have to pay costs to my client. (You should check your jurisdiction's Court Rules to see what the consequences are in your circumstances). Ultimately, you will want this letter to impress a judge with your patience and reasonableness in the face of the other side's foot-dragging.

2. When the deadline passes, send another letter advising the other side that your deadline has been missed and that you are now preparing to go to court, and that you will file a motion by a second deadline. Make this deadline shorter. For example, ten days from the date of the letter. Begin to research and prepare a motion (see Chapter 6).

3. If you have not received the documents, you will likely have to evaluate whether it is worth the time and effort to make a Motion to Court. If there is clear noncompliance and you know they possess information or a document that is going to be admissible and relevant at trial, a motion may be a good idea.

4. If the other side, instead of not complying, offers a document here, a more comprehensive interrogatory answer there you will be left wondering whether it is worth the time and energy

to make a motion to court to demand that the other side follow discovery rules. After all, they have supplied some of the information, but not all. Sadly, this is a typical situation for a litigation file. I am constantly weighing the value of not filing a motion and saving time and expense versus not having the information and whether this will hurt my client at trial. Ultimately, you will have to make the call. This may be a time to try to consult a lawyer for a legal opinion. Or if you have another motion or matter before the Court (e.g., you have to go to court for an injunction to preserve property), you may want to mention this. (Though the Court might tell you that this is not proper as you should file a motion. Situations such as a pre-trial conference would, however, be an appropriate time to say that discovery has been hindered by the other side.)

6
Motions and Temporary Orders

Odds are that if you're holding this book and are involved in a court case, that you have or will participate in a motion hearing. Odds are also that you will not participate in a trial. In my view, this is probably the most important chapter in this book and understanding how to succeed at a motion is the skill that will pay you the biggest dividends.

Trials take a long time to actually happen. From the time you file and serve the other side (or you are served) to the time you have a trial, it may take from six months to several years. In that time period there may be situations that need resolving that you need to ask a judge to make a decision on, ranging from procedural complications with your case such as when you are not able to serve the court case on the other side, to emergencies where quick action is needed to prevent some harm (such as a restraining order to prevent disposal of property).

It is not uncommon to make a request for the Court to make an order telling the other party to do something before trial. A request for such an order is typically called a "motion," "pre-trial motion," "inter-locutory application," or a "request for temporary orders." The order made at a motion hearing is considered temporary because the decision a judge makes at a full trial is the final order and takes precedence over any orders made prior to the trial. Orders made at a motion hearing may also be called "interlocutory orders" or "interim orders."

Motions may be made in one of these ways:

- In writing and decided without a hearing.

- In writing and decided at a hearing.

- Entirely orally, in open court, without anything in writing.

The typical way to make a motion in court follows these steps:

1. One party files and serves a Notice of Motion setting out what he or she wants the court to do with, usually, an attached affidavit providing evidence.

2. The other side may or may not file a response to the motion with their own affidavit and evidence.

3. The parties attend a motion hearing. Generally, these hearings are short (from 5 to 30 minutes) and there are no witnesses. (Motions for restraining orders, however, often have oral testimony from a witness.) A jury is never present at a motion hearing. Each side has a turn to present their reasons for making the motion or objecting to it.

4. The judge either makes an order "from the bench" right away or takes the matter "under advisement" and makes a written order later.

Motions can be a critical stage of litigation. In fact, you may be able to dismiss the other side's entire case by winning certain motions. Because most cases never end up going to trial, a motion might be the pivotal moment in winning, losing, or settling your case. I like to think of any motion, no matter how small, as a skirmish in a greater war. Some are more important than others. Some may even win the war. That being said, if you do end up having a trial, your trial judge isn't going to keep track of how many motions you've won and lost. Your trial judge will not keep score with respect to the hearings that have happened before.

1. Common Motions

Motions vary from requests for orders that are very similar to the order that you might end up with at trial, to orders that help move the court process along. Because a motion is just another word for a request to the Court there are potentially hundreds of kinds of motions you can make. The Court must have the jurisdiction and power to make the order you are requesting.

With respect to motions, the Court generally will want to see a reason why the matter is coming before the Court now rather than waiting for trial. That's the big difference between what you ask for in a motion and at trial. What you ask for in a motion must have some element of urgency and needing to be addressed sooner rather than later.

Thus the following motions can be grouped into two categories: Urgent/emergency motions and procedural motions that affect the process of preparing for trial and need to be taken care of to keep the trial on track. Both involve the resolution of something that needs to be dealt with sooner rather than later.

1.1 Urgent motions

There are circumstances where you will need to ask for a court to order some part of the relief you are asking for in your claim before a trial. Typically these orders seek to preserve what is commonly referred to as the status quo. In other words, they are meant to preserve the situation as it currently is. Orders that preserve the status quo are known as injunctive relieve or restraining orders. (Yes, restraining orders can be made outside of family violence situations to restrain some sort of conduct.) They tell a party to do or not do something.

The following is a non-exhaustive list of examples of circumstances where you will want to consider going to court for a motion:

- **Motion to preserve property:** Property is at risk of being disposed of or destroyed. For example, you allege that you are a partner in a business. Your partner is trying to sell business assets. To prevent sale of the business assets before trial you will need a court order restraining your partner from selling them (or, if the Court will not grant that order, an order that your partner must retain proceeds from the sale in trust until a final court order).

- **Motion for injunctive relief to preserve status quo:** The other party is about to do something that is at issue in the claim. For example, let's say the defendant is about to develop a piece of property. You are suing to prevent development. If there is a risk that the developer is about to start, you will need to ask the Court to stop the developer from developing the land before the trial.

Family law especially lends itself to urgent need for a court order:

- **Motion for child support:** If a child is not receiving child support and should be, this is a reason to ask the Court for an order sooner rather than later.

- **Motion for spousal support:** Similarly, if your legal research indicates that you are eligible for spousal support, you may want to consider getting into court earlier rather than later. Be careful to research the law carefully as this is a tricky area.

- **Motion for child custody/parenting time and visitation:** Though motions to increase parenting time are very common in family law proceedings, this is a complicated area of law which generally focuses on what is best for the child or children involved. In my experience, a court will not increase parenting time from the status quo (i.e., from an established routine) unless there is a good reason to do so. A good reason might include when the other parent's parenting ability changes (this is unusual but can happen due to, for example, health issues) or if there is some harm to the child with the current status quo. Another situation where a court may intervene is in circumstances where one parent abruptly changes a child's parenting time with another parent. Courts may require expert evidence at these kinds of hearings.

- **Motion for a restraining order:** Restraining orders often can be started as their own action or they can be a temporary order made by motion as part of another case (this is known as an underlying action) such as a divorce. If you are experiencing or fear some form of violence, you should contact the police. After making sure that you and your family are safe, I recommend that you speak to a lawyer. Victims of family violence may be eligible for legal aid and should consider contacting support services such as crisis hotlines, shelters, and family and friends. If you do need to obtain a restraining order but choose not to contact the police, there is sometimes a victim support worker or equivalent assistance at your local courthouse. Typically, restraining orders involving family violence are obtained *ex parte*, meaning without notice to the other side.

1.1a Getting an order without letting the other side know: What does *ex parte* mean?

Ex parte simply means one side only. So, a hearing that is *ex parte* means that only one side knows about the hearing and is at the hearing.

It is a principle of the fairness of our court system that both parties should have notice of a hearing and an opportunity to attend that hearing. *Ex parte* hearings permit the Court to override this requirement in urgent situations. If you want an *ex parte* hearing, you will have to explain to the Court why it is important to dispense with notice of the hearing to the other side. Because *ex parte* hearings violate due process, orders made at them are usually only temporary and will expire by a certain date. You can come back to the court hearing with notice to the other side to request that the temporary order continue.

Courts do not like to make *ex parte* orders without good reason. It is not a good idea to apply for one just because you think you'll have a better chance of winning if the other side is not there.

During *ex parte* hearings, lawyers often have a duty to tell the court about information that actually may hurt their case. (In a normal court hearing a lawyer does not have to do this. It is up to the other side to point out the weaknesses of the lawyer's case.)

Here are examples of *ex parte* hearings:

- **Family violence restraining orders:** These orders are commonly referred to as "TRO," which stands for Temporary Restraining Order.

- **Irreparable harm:** If one party is about to cause some harm that cannot be undone, it may be necessary to get into court quickly to prevent that harm. For example, to protect property that is about to be sold or there is evidence that the other side is going to move your children out of the jurisdiction.

1.1b Can I shorten the notice requirement? Short notice

In urgent situations that are not as serious as *ex parte* motions, you may ask the court to shorten or otherwise change the notice requirements to let the other side know about a hearing (e.g., from seven to four days). As short notice gives the other side less time to get ready for court, there must be a good reason, unless, of course, if the other side agrees to shorten the notice requirement.

1.2 Procedural motions

The following are some procedural motions:

- **Motion to dismiss:** This is a request to the Court to dismiss the claims of a party because of some deficiency in the claims. Basically, it is a request for the Court to stop a court case because for some reason the case is not properly brought. It is not the same as asking the Court to not believe the claims asserted. In fact, a successful motion to dismiss will work even if all the claims of the other side were true. Unlike most other motions, this motion is asking the Court to make a final decision. Here are some examples of motions to dismiss:

- **Statute of limitations has expired:** In cases where there was a time limit to bring the lawsuit, and it is brought after that time limit has expired, a motion to dismiss the case could be made. This motion would only look at whether or not the statute of limitations has been exceeded and, if so, there is some legal reason to still permit the case to go ahead. (Understanding limitations can be very confusing. Take care to learn the limitations involved in your case. For example, in British Columbia, a new *Limitation Act* went into force on June 1, 2013. However, the old *Limitation Act* still applies if the act or omission giving rise to a civil claim occurred and was discovered prior to June 1, 2013.)

- **Failure to assert a valid legal claim:** If the other side's claims ask for relief for something without any legal foundation, you could make a Motion for Failure to Assert a Valid Legal Claim. For example, let's say that your candy store stopped stocking your favourite candy and so you sued them. The candy store has no duty to provide the candy you like. Therefore, the candy store should be able to dismiss your claim as not legally valid.

- **Lack of jurisdiction:** This would include situations were the other side has, for example, filed their case in the wrong court.

- **Motion to amend pleadings:** There are generally specific rules about whether and how often you can change court papers that you have already filed. If you notice a mistake in your pleadings, especially if you fail to ask for something that you should have, it is a good idea to consider amending your pleadings. Depending on your jurisdiction, you may be able to amend your pleadings once if you do so early enough in the case without needing to make a motion.

- **Motion for discovery:** If you have not received discovery, Court Rules generally permit you to ask the Court to order that the other side provide discovery to you within a certain period of time. If you have not received answers to interrogatories, your motion is called a Motion to Compel.

- **Motion for injunction:** An injunction is an order which requires the other side to do or not do something.

- **Motion for substituted or alternative service:** If the person who is to be served is evading service or is difficult to serve, you can ask the Court for an order allowing you to serve him or her by another method.

- **Motion for summary judgment:** Like a motion to dismiss, the motion for summary judgment can be a shortcut to winning your case. It is also a request to the Court to make a final decision. Of all the motions listed here, this is the one most easily misunderstood, the most technical, and which will require you to do substantial legal research and thinking.

  The basic principle is that there must not be any material fact in dispute. In other words, you and the other side must agree on the relevant facts that prove or disprove the claims. If you both agree, then what we have left is a purely legal dispute about what the law says should be done about the agreed-upon facts. For example, let's say that a contract said that a home renovation had to be completed "by" one year of the date of signing the contract or the contractor would have to offer a significant discount on the work. The contract was signed on November 1, 2015. The work was completed on November 1, 2016. The plaintiff and defendant agree on this. The only argument is therefore about the meaning of the contract, especially the word "by." This is purely a question of law. The way the contractor can fight a motion for summary judgment is to say there are issues of fact that need to be looked at; for example, maybe the parties differ on whether all the work was completed. If there really are issues of fact in dispute, a judge will deny a motion for summary judgment so that the parties can test the facts at a full trial.

- **Motion to postpone or continue a hearing date:** It may happen that a hearing is scheduled on a date that is impossible or difficult for you to attend. Your first step should be to see if the other side will agree to a new date. If there is no urgency in the matter and no history of delay in the case by either party, courts generally expect that the parties will be flexible about rescheduling hearing dates, especially the first time. If the other side agrees, you will have to check with the court registry about what paperwork may be required to reschedule the hearing. (For example, some courts require a letter while others will want a motion with both parties signatures on file). If the other side does not agree, you will have to file a motion to change the hearing date.

- **Motion for sanctions:** If you believe the other side is intentionally delaying the case or subverting the court process (e.g., by repeatedly not providing discovery by required deadlines or providing incomplete discovery, or asking for continuances simply to delay the case), you can ask the Court to sanction them. A sanction is a penalty, usually a fine, imposed by a judge on a party for not following Court Rules. In my experience, it is unusual to make such a motion but not unusual to warn the other side that if they don't start complying with court rules you will have to make such a motion.

1.3 Getting ready for motions in writing

Try to avoid a non-emergency motion by negotiating first. You should usually communicate with the other side about reaching agreement on the issue on which you will be filing a motion. (In some jurisdictions this is required.) For example, if the Court schedules a pre-trial hearing date that you cannot attend, ask the other side if they would agree to change that date before you file a motion for continuance. Or if you are about to make a motion for child support, talk to the other side because they may want to avoid the time and expense of a hearing and agree to temporarily pay support until the trial.

In my practice, I start with a phone call and, if that doesn't work, I try to set up an in-person meeting. If that doesn't work, the next step is a letter explaining my client's position and what we want. I then explain that if a resolution is not found by a certain date, that I will have to file a motion. Often, a letter may lead to another round of negotiation by phone or letter. However, if that appears to not be working, then I go ahead and file a motion.

If you reach agreement with the other side about procedural issues that affect the court (e.g., scheduling issues or deadlines imposed by the Court), you will need to let the Court know about the agreement. A common way to do this is usually by preparing and filing a motion that is "by consent." That means that the other side agrees to what you are asking the Court to do.

Alternately, if the agreement doesn't affect court procedure, you might not need to file a motion and may want to record your agreement in a written temporary agreement. Knowing when to make a motion by consent and when a written agreement is sufficient is a choice that will depend on your kind of case, your jurisdiction, and the court you are in. (Checking with a lawyer is a good idea.)

If you are in doubt, or believe that a court order is appropriate, it may be prudent to appear before the Court to tell the Court about the agreement. This is most easily done by filing a motion by consent. When you make a motion by consent you should attach a draft of the order you and the other side have agreed on. Some jurisdictions call this a "stipulation."

You should write on your motion that it is "by consent" and have the other party either sign the motion as agreed to or, when you go to court to have the motion heard, tell the Court that the other side is in agreement with you. The Court will be relieved to not have to hear you and the other side arguing about the motion. However, the Court reserves the right to not approve the motion. In my experience, the court will almost always approve a consented to motion that is fair and reasonable, though I do see the court sometimes making small changes with respect to:

1. Logistical problems, or whether you can actually do what the order says. For example, if the proposed order says you are going to pay $10,000 by 5:00 p.m. that day, the Court may ask if it is possible for you to actually obtain this sum of money in such short order.

2. The wording of the order to make sure it is consistent and clear. For example, an order that says the plaintiff will drop off the children on Tuesdays might concern a court because it is not specific enough: It doesn't say where or what time the children will be dropped off.

   If no agreement is reached by negotiating, prepare the materials for your motion.

1.4 Drafting the notice of motion

Court Rules generally do set out the format for a notice of motion. Frequently, you will be able to find the appropriate form on your court's website. Or you may be able to obtain one from the court registry. If there is no form that you can either fill in or copy, you will have to see if your Court Rules contain an example. You might also find examples on legal aid websites for your jurisdiction or in law books and manuals at the local law library.

What you put in the motion (the content) will depend on how complicated the motion is. A very simple motion such as a motion for continuance by consent might be as simple as a couple of sentences explaining the background to the request, what you and the other side have agreed upon and requesting that the court reschedule to the new agreed upon date. See Motion for Continuance by Consent, included on the download kit that came with this book.

For more complicated motions, the typical elements are:

- A brief summary of the facts: These facts must come from evidence. Typically, that evidence comes from the motion's supporting affidavit. Usually, I write the supporting affidavit first and then summarize the essential facts as briefly as possible in the motion. Do not argue your case in the description of facts. The way I like to think of the facts section of a motion is that they will be completely stripped of any emotion or argument and because they are so straightforward, that a judge reading them will logically start to come round to my client's point of view.

- A brief summary of the relevant statutes and any case law: In my practice I try to do two things in this area: Be specific (don't just cite "the *Consumer Protection Act*," rather cite specific sections if you know them) and, if it is not too lengthy, write out the relevant law. (Bring photocopies of the law to the hearing to show the judge.) Don't cite ten cases on a simple motion. Instead, if the law is subject to interpretation, cite the leading case and one or two cases that are similar to your case.

- What you want the court to do: Otherwise known as "relief." Think of this section as the conclusion. The facts are already pointing to what you want the Court to do and the law is there to give the judge permission to do what you want.

See the download kit for example wording for some motions.

2. Estimating Time

Court Rules may require you to estimate how long the motion hearing will take on the Notice of Motion form. How do you do this? Typically, motions do not involve witnesses. Evidence is only what is in the affidavits and attached documents filed with your motion.

Practice your motion and time yourself. Be concise! Typically, motions range from five minutes to one hour. Once you've timed yourself, you should double that time to allow for the other side's counterargument. Generally, if you know that the motion will be opposed, you should allow at least 20 minutes.

Don't worry if your estimate isn't exact. (I've never been held to an estimate; however, I do tend to be brief.) Really, the purpose of this estimate is for court staff to know how to schedule your motion; typically shorter motions go before longer motions. Generally:

- When the other side and I are presenting a motion where all the parties have consented, I say the motion will be five minutes total.

- When a motion involves only one affidavit and is relatively straightforward without complicated law, I say 20 minutes.

- When a motion involves a couple of affidavits and is more complicated, I estimate from 20 minutes to an hour.

- If there are multiple parties, multiple affidavits, and the facts and law are very complicated, I generally try to talk to the other side about trying to find some agreement on issues so that the court is not overwhelmed, and I try to get a sense from them as to whether we can agree on a time estimate.

3. Drafting an Affidavit for a Motion

An affidavit is a written statement which you swear or affirm to be true. Depending on your jurisdiction, you may have to swear your affidavit before a notary public or a lawyer. Affidavits typically are divided into short, numbered paragraphs. Often, documents are attached to the affidavit, called "exhibits," and are given letters of the alphabet to identify them in the affidavit (e.g., Exhibit A). Affidavit forms and examples may be available from the court's website, or from legal aid providers in your jurisdiction.

The purpose of an affidavit for a motion is to provide the evidence you will be relying on. There are limited circumstances where you may not need an affidavit for your motion. For example:

1. If you and the other side agree on the motion so that it is "by consent." You will be able to provide supporting evidence by telling the Court what the terms of settlement are when you are in court.

2. You will be relying on oral testimony (i.e., witnesses) at the motion hearing. It will depend on your jurisdiction as to whether this is allowed.

For example, in family law matters in BC Provincial Court many self-represented parties do not attach affidavits and instead make oral testimony in court.

I recommend erring on the side of caution and preparing an affidavit anyway in the above two situations unless you are 100 percent certain that an affidavit is not needed.

The most important thing to remember about drafting an affidavit is that it is sworn testimony, just like testimony in court. Be careful to provide honest, accurate information. If you are not 100 percent sure about a fact, say so. You do not want to give the other side the opportunity to say that you are lying and thus not credible. Worse, knowingly swearing a false affidavit is a criminal offence in Canada (see s.131 of the Criminal Code).

3.1 Parts of an affidavit

Check your jurisdiction's rules for the elements necessary for an affidavit. However, the following are common elements:

- Name of the proceeding/style of cause. Like a notice of motion and most papers filed in court, the first page should include the names of the parties, the name of the court, and the docket number. The affidavit should be titled by the name of the person swearing it (the deponent; for example, "Affidavit of Mary Jane").

- An affidavit is written as if you are the person signing it. In other words, it is in the first person and will begin with "I." So, if you are writing an affidavit for a witness, you will write it as if that person were speaking. Use language that that person would normally use. An introductory paragraph will orient the Court as to who is testifying. Generally, that means providing the person's name, address, and occupation. The beginning usually also contains some boilerplate phrase that indicates that the affidavit is sworn testimony. For example, if Mark Torri is the plaintiff in the case and is a sales clerk, then his affidavit's introductory paragraph might read, "I, Mark Torri, sales clerk, of 321 Pembroke St, Victoria, British Columbia, affirm that I am the Plaintiff in this matter and have personal knowledge of the matters herein referred to." In BC, an affidavit must be concluded by signing it in front of a notary public or lawyer. Paragraphs are numbered.

- Generally, you should stick to the facts as you or the deponent know them in an affidavit. For example, "I saw a blue vehicle enter the intersection." However, there are times that you will need to convey information of which you do not have firsthand knowledge. For example, when someone tells you that a blue vehicle entered the intersection and you want to put this in the affidavit. (This is generally considered hearsay but may be allowed such as in BC in interlocutory civil motions.) You should provide the source of the information. You should also begin the paragraph with the wording: "On information and belief … ."

  For example, let's say that you are seeking an order to prevent the other side from felling a tree that is jointly on your property line. You have learned that the other side recently purchased a chainsaw. You learned this from a clerk at a hardware store. Ideally, you would have a sworn statement (i.e., an affidavit) from the clerk. If you are unable to obtain one, your next best option would be to include a statement as follows: "On information and belief, the Defendant purchased on approximately September 1, 20XX, a chainsaw from Foxglove Hardware. I believe this to be true because I spoke with Ian Foxglove, owner and manager at Foxglove Hardware on March 15, 20XX, and he informed me of this."

- Keep the affidavit short and simple. Judges like clarity and essential information only. Stick to the facts and don't add opinions. Sometimes, in family law proceedings, an opinion can be helpful to illustrate, for example, parenting styles, but it is important to remember that you cannot provide expert opinion if you are not an expert. That, and the ultimate issues — who should win the case — are issues for the judge, not the person swearing an affidavit.

- The best order for paragraphs in an affidavit is almost always chronological. Give exact dates if you can. For example, February 15, 2000, is ideal; mid-February 2000 is good; February 2000 is okay; and winter 2000 is better than "sometime in 2000" although that beats "about 15 years ago." Also, when talking about people, try to use the person's name rather than "him" or "her," which can be confusing.

- Make sure that the affidavit is internally consistent. If you said that you were approximately 20 feet away from the intersection in one paragraph but in another that you were at the intersection, you have a problem that needs to be explained.

- Also, if there are other affidavits you have made, make sure this affidavit is consistent with those affidavits. (Personally, when I am working a file, I am delighted to find that the other side has contradicted themselves in multiple affidavits. Suddenly that deponent's credibility is not looking so good.)

- If you make a mistake, remember, everyone, lawyers included, make mistakes. It's what we do about them afterwards that counts. If you discover after filing and serving an affidavit that it contains false or misleading information, don't panic. In my practice, I generally would ask the deponent if they knowingly made a false statement or misled me. If they did so, well, then I probably would stop representing them. More commonly, a client will discover that, for example, their bank records indicate a different figure than they swore to, or they will reread the affidavit and discover their is a typo or they will think back and decide that they aren't really sure whether the car that hit them was blue because it might have been green. If something like this happens, my first recommendation is to talk to a lawyer because the facts of your case are unique and a general book such as this cannot anticipate all the facts. I do not recommend doing nothing, however. A second step may be to prepare a corrected version of the affidavit, reswear it, and file it as a corrected version. Do not simply write over the incorrect affidavit without initialing any change and re-swearing (signing again). A letter explaining the error to the other side is also a practice I have employed in the past.

4. Exhibits

Sometimes you will need a specific document to be introduced as evidence to support your motion. For example, if your motion is partially based on the fact that you and the defendant signed a written contract, you can attach that contract to your affidavit. You would reference it as: "Attached to this my affidavit as Exhibit A is a true copy of the contract between Dan Dunning and myself dated March 15, 20XX." You should not necessarily describe the contents of the document (e.g., what the contract between Dan Dunning and you says) as the document speaks for itself. However, it is helpful to highlight why you are attaching it.

When you attach a copy of the document, you will need to mark it with an exhibit letter starting with Exhibit A and the next Exhibit B and so on. (Lawyers use a stamp to do this.) You can just write "Exhibit A" clearly on the attached copy of the document. Usually, each exhibit requires the signature of the notary. Check local practice rules for how this is done in your jurisdiction and court.

Exhibits will be subject to the rules of evidence. Thus, it will be up to the judge to decide if they are admissible or not. Typically, these rules are less strictly imposed on urgent motions. You should check the rules and law in your jurisdiction.

5. Drafting a Draft Order

Depending on your jurisdiction, you may be required to provide a draft order when you file your Notice of Motion. Drafting an order is challenging. I do not recommend that a self-represented person do so without legal assistance. However, I understand that sometimes an unrepresented person will simply have to do it himself or herself.

If you win your hearing, you will need to clarify whether the court will draft your order. Typically, in my experience, courts do not expect unrepresented parties to draft an order after a hearing. Usually, the court clerk will use their notes to draft an order or, if the other side is represented, their lawyer will draft the order. If the other side's lawyer drafts the order, it may be sent to you for your approval as to form only. This is not an opportunity to argue with that lawyer about the judge's decision, only to make sure the wording the lawyer used accurately and fairly reflects the order the judge made in court. If there is any uncertainty about an order and what the judge ordered, the court registry may be able to assist. Usually, the clerk sitting in court will have taken notes of the terms of the order. Also, court hearings are recorded and it may be possible for you to listen to the hearing or order a hearing transcript.

Sometimes you may have to file a draft order ahead of your hearing because it is required by Court Rules.

As a lawyer, I always draft an order for a motion hearing, even if it not required. I bring to the hearing a draft order for the judge to sign right away if I win in court. I like to have one on hand (or filed if the registry requires or allows that) to make it as easy as possible for the court to side with my client. For example, at the conclusion of my oral argument, I will generally offer the judge a copy of my draft order to look over. Sometimes this helps a decision maker clearly understand what it is I am seeking. A draft order also serves as a checklist for me at the end of my oral argument: I scan my draft order to make sure I have articulated reasons for each of my requests and have not failed to ask for something.

Keep in mind, if you win, and the judge decides to sign your draft order, that draft will become an enforceable and binding Order of the Court. Great care must be taken in getting the terms of that order right.

Make sure that if your jurisdiction requires a certain form or format, that you have that. Give the order a title. For example, "Order for Child Support." Describe who attended the hearing. For example, you will set out your name and say that you appeared *pro se* or "unrepresented." Next, look at the relief you have requested in your Notice of Motion. You will want to repeat that but in the imperative language of a court order. Use similar language to other orders made by the Court. For example, in your motion you may request: "Disclosure of all credit card statements of the Plaintiff for last three years to be delivered to the Defendant on or before March 15, 20XX." In asking for your Order you should proposes how and when this should happen and the Order should reflect what the Court specified: "The Defendant will deliver to the Plaintiff photocopies of all the Defendant's credit card statements for the period of time from March 1, 2012, to March 15, 2015, by March 15, 2016.

If the order requires payment to you, state when the payment will be made and how it will be made (i.e., money order or cheque). Do not assume that a lack of clarity or vagueness means that things will get done. Vagueness may create a situation where the other side does not know how to follow the order as well as make it hard to enforce the order.

6. Scheduling, Filing, Service

When it comes to scheduling a motion hearing, figure out how much notice you must give the other side (be liberal). For example, if you must give seven days notice, factor in when you actually think the other side will be served (it may take longer than you expect) and then add several days in case they don't get served, and that is the earliest date for your hearing. Next, you will have to figure out what dates the Court is available to hear the motion.

I have practiced law in three different jurisdictions and at scores of courthouses and administrative agencies. How you get a date before a judge varies widely. Your best bet is to talk to the registry staff and find out from them how a hearing is scheduled. Take notes of what the registry staff tell you. For example, in BC, to schedule a hearing before the Supreme Court, my office would phone the Court and the Court staff would schedule the motion into the docket. Then, we would file and serve the Notice of Motion with the scheduled date clearly set out on the Notice of Motion. Generally, I will check with the lawyer on the other side before scheduling a motion to make sure they are available on that date. Because you are self-represented, it is possible that a non-represented person or a lawyer who is not as courteous as I am will take advantage of your request for their available dates and rush into court to schedule their own motion hearing before yours, thus perhaps gaining the upper hand. In my experience, this is very rare, but if you are concerned that the other side might in fact do this, you should consider filing and setting the hearing date without checking with the other side.

6.1 Responding to a filed and served written motion

If you receive a Notice of Motion, read it carefully. It will probably give a date and time for a hearing. Mark that in your calendar.

It may also set out a time limit for you to file and serve a response (also called a "reply," an "opposition," or some other name) to the motion. If the motion does not set out when you must file a response, you should check the Court Rules to figure out if there is a deadline. If you do not meet this deadline, the Court might determine that you have consented to the motion.

Your reply to a Notice of Motion should either agree or disagree with what the other side is asking for. Explain your reasons for disagreeing by setting out the facts as you see them.

If you do not respond or do not show up at the motion hearing date, the Court could make an order against you. You may also decide to make your own motion, which you will have to file and serve on the other side, as well as set down for hearing, as required by your jurisdiction's Court Rules.

Ensure the motion served on you complies with Court Rules. If the other side did not properly serve you with the motion (e.g., they emailed it to you when Court Rules require service by regular mail), you might be able to ask the Court to have it dismissed.

Like the party starting a motion, the person responding to a motion can also file affidavits and documents for the Court to consider. In fact, if you disagree with a motion, you should file an affidavit in response setting out your version of the facts.

Frequently, when served with an affidavit, a party will spend time pouring over every detail of that affidavit and become quiet angry and upset by it. I can recall numerous times that a client has come to me with an affidavit that has been served on him or her that my client has covered with notes. At this point, the litigation can go one of two ways: An affidavit war is started where each side attacks every detail in the other side's affidavit, or the sides tell their stories the natural way they would tell someone who knows nothing about the dispute, sticking to what is relevant.

The second way is the way to win a motion hearing.

Check your Court Rules regarding evidence on motions. If your jurisdiction permits, one way to address statements the other side's affidavit makes but avoid nitpicking every statement is to say something to the effect of:

"I will be responding to the allegations of fact contained in the claimant's Affidavit #15 that are relevant to the issues to be determined on this motion. My failure to respond to each of the allegations should not be construed as an admission of the accuracy of any of the allegations."

It remains important to deny statements of fact that are relevant to the issues at hand and with which you disagree. See "Avoiding Affidavit Wars" on the download kit included with this book for helpful tips.

6.2 How do you present a filed and served motion in court?

Motions may be decided with or without a hearing. If your motion is set for a hearing, you should expect to present oral argument to the court about why your evidence supports the relief you are requesting.

The most important thing you can do to succeed at your motion is to have a well-prepared case when you walk into the courtroom.

When you arrive at court, check the docket to make sure your case is listed for today and check what courtroom it is in. Your case may have been given a number. Jot down that number on your pad of paper because when you check in the clerk may ask for it. Also, your case may be called out for hearing by that number.

Check in with the clerk. In many courts, it is common practice for lawyers and unrepresented parties to line up in the assigned courtroom before the hearing time (I usually show up at least 20 minutes early) to check in with the judge's clerk, who will want to know if the motion is going ahead or if the matter was settled, and if all the parties are present.

Wait in the courtroom. Often, dozens of motions are set for the same time. The court clerk will have to sort through which hearings can go first. Usually, any hearings that have settled get to go first. The judge will listen to the terms of the settlement and approve or suggest changes for the terms of the order, or deny the settlement.

Waiting is an opportunity to see how other parties handle procedure. It might also give you a hint as to what the judge likes and doesn't like.

The clerk or judge will call your case. For example, "Number 42, Jones versus Jones. Motion for an Injunction." Approach the bench. You will usually stand at one of the two tables in front of the judge's desk. Do not sit down yet!

It is up to the judge to decide how a motion proceeds. In my experience, judges usually follow the following steps for a motion hearing and will usually interrupt at some point with questions. Your job is to think of the judge as someone you need to politely and clearly provide with information.

If you are the party bringing the motion, introduce yourself. For example, if I had brought a Motion for Discovery I would say, "Good morning, Your Honour. My name is Devlin Farmer and I am self-represented. This is my motion for discovery."

After the moving party (the party who made the motion) has introduced themselves, it's the other party's turn. Even if the other side has spoken for awhile (they really should only introduce themselves), make sure you let the judge know who you are and what your position is on the motion. "Good morning Your Honour. My name is Devlin Farmer and I'm self-represented. I am in disagreement with this motion. It is my position that discovery has been completed."

The next steps will vary depending on whether the judge has read the supporting material and the judge's style. Sometimes a judge may want to put you under oath to provide evidence. Or you may want to do this if you have not provided any other sworn evidence (i.e., an affidavit). If you testify, keep it short and as specific as possible. The other side will have an opportunity to cross-examine you. See more about cross-examination in Chapter 9.

The next step is the "argument." The moving party goes first and explains their motion and introduces any evidence. The approach I take is to do a combination of explaining the evidence in a summary format (this will hold the judge's attention better than reading out an entire affidavit or document to the Court) and highlighting key evidence by turning directly to the a sentence or part of a document in the materials. Expect questions from the judge. Once you're done tell the judge what the order is that you are asking for.

Next, it will be up to the responding party to explain their opposition and introduce their evidence (in the same manner as the moving party).

Both parties can ask for an opportunity to respond to what the other side has said.

The judge will either make a decision "from the bench" right away or will reserve and make a written decision that you will receive in the mail. During the court hearing you should see yourself as the judge's guide through the evidence. Prepare for this job by writing an outline of how you are going to guide the judge through the evidence. See the download kit for an example of Walking the Court through Your Motion.

Organizing Your Material

I recommend making an index of the material you are bringing with you to court so that it is easy to find. (Assume that you will be dumbstruck in court and unable to find things.) If your jurisdiction does not require placing the motion material in a binder (e.g., in BC Supreme Court this is required), I suggest placing your material in a three-ring binder with tabs. (I make three copies of everything that I think the judge might want to see. One for myself, one for the other side, and one for the judge. Although the judge should have the file including all pleadings, I go into the hearing assuming that the file has not found its way to the judge because that does happen and being ready for that gives you a leg up.) There is an example of an index for a typical motion hearing in the download kit.

7. Courtroom Etiquette

Courtrooms can be overwhelming places. The lawyers all seem to know each other and what they are doing. Things happen either very quickly or very slowly. If you feel overwhelmed, don't worry. So do a lot of other people in the courtroom.

Being nervous is normal. In fact, I see it as an advantage: It means you take the proceedings seriously and will have put the preparation in that is needed to successfully win your case. (A person who is not nervous is less likely to take precautions such as writing down what to say or making checklists.)

That said, here are some tips so you know what to do:

- Dress professionally. Never wear a T-shirt or anything with writing on it. Avoid anything that might draw attention to yourself such as costly jewellery. You want to appear plain, tidy, and most importantly, polite.

- When you arrive, after checking in with the clerk, sit in the body of the courtroom. The front row of seats is usually reserved for lawyers. (In most courtrooms, the seats inside a wooden gate or "bar" are for lawyers. Thus the term "passing" the bar refers to passing that wooden fence.) When your case is called, you generally will stand before one of two tables in front of the clerk's desk and the judge's desk. If your motion is short, you will probably remain standing. If you need to sit down for health reasons, tell the judge that you would like to sit down and explain why. If your motion is longer, you may sit down during the other side's presentation. Usually the judge will signal to you when you can sit down. If you are able, you should always stand when speaking to the judge.

- Don't interrupt the judge or the other side. If you object to something the other side is saying, make a note and make sure you come back to that. If you feel you really should interrupt (e.g., if the other side is reciting agreed upon facts incorrectly), stand and wait until the judge addresses you.

- Don't argue with the other side or their lawyer. Your job is to persuade the judge, not the other side. You should direct everything you say to the judge.

- It's okay to ask questions of the judge about procedure (e.g., what happens next?) if you aren't sure. In fact, lawyers do this too. If you are unsure what is supposed to happen next or what your options are, politely ask the judge for direction. Let the judge know what you would like. While a judge cannot provide legal advice or advocate, he or she can and should help unrepresented persons with questions of procedure.

- Court Rules and the law are complicated and there may come a situation that you don't understand but which feels unfair. For example, let's say that the other side tells the Court that they have a report from an expert that they would like to show the Court. You aren't sure what the law is about experts but wonder what is in the report. You would like to see it. You tell the Court that you haven't seen the report. The other side says that it was disclosed to you. Is that the end of the story? No. You should tell the judge that you did not receive the report and do not feel it is fair for them to rely on a document that you haven't seen. You should ask for proof that it was disclosed to you and, even if there is proof, you should ask for time to read the report.

8. How Do You Make an Oral Motion When the Trial Has Already Started?

The time for motions at a trial is usually at the very beginning. Or, if the need for a motion rises up during the trial, you should let the Court know as soon as you can that you would like to make the motion. It is always up the judge to decide when he or she will hear the motion. Here's how a motion may look after the case has been called and the parties introduced themselves:

Plaintiff: Your Honour, I'd like to make a make a motion that today's hearing either be adjourned or, if that is not allowed, that my witness, Mr. John Edgar, be permitted to testify by telephone.

Judge: Have you given notice of this motion to the defendant?

Plaintiff: Your Honour, I let the defendant know this morning as soon as I discovered that Mr. Edgar could not come to court today. Unfortunately, I only learned that he could not come this morning.

Defendant: That's right. I've just found out and I think the trial needs to go ahead today.

Judge: OK. I'll hear your reasons for the motion Mr. Plaintiff, and then I'll hear from you, Mr. Defendant.

Plaintiff: Your Honour, Mr. Edgar is the only witness who saw the accident. He was present at the supermarket when I slipped and fell. Four weeks ago, on March 18, 20XX, I served a subpoena on Mr. Edgar to appear in Court today. Mr. Edgar telephoned me at 8:15 this morning. He told me that he had been in a car accident yesterday and was taken to Montgomery Hospital where he learned that he had suffered whiplash. He was discharged that evening. He told me that the doctor told him to stay at home resting today and not to drive anywhere. I am asking the Court to continue this trial to a new date so that Mr. Edgar can testify. He is essential to my case because I know the Defendant will say that the floor was marked by a warning sign. Mr. Edgar will testify that it was not. Alternately, if the Court will not adjourn the trial, I would request that Mr. Edgar be permitted to testify by telephone.

Judge: Thank you. And you have Mr. Edgar's telephone number?

Plaintiff: Yes.

Judge: If that is all, I'll now hear from the Defendant.

Defendant: Your Honour, I have taken the entire day off work today. My witness has also taken the entire day off work. We have been waiting eight months for this trial. Delay will cost me more money. I do not know if my witness will be available on a new trial date.

Judge: What about if Mr. Edgar testified by phone?

Defendant: How can I show him the picture of the warning sign? If he is only on the phone, you will not be able to see his face and know if he is telling the truth or not.

Judge: Anything further? No? Thank you.

I expect that the judge would probably allow the adjournment if it was the first request.

8.1 Typical oral motions in court

During a hearing or trial, circumstances may come up that you want the court to do something about. Let's say that a witness continues to testify about hearsay statements despite your successful objections. Those statements are going to go into the trial transcript and, if there is an appeal, you probably don't want them to be seen. You'll want to ask the judge to do something about that. Or let's say, the other side has introduced a piece of evidence you've never seen before but which you don't want to object to because it looks like it helps your case. You'll want the judge to give you time to review that evidence and adjourn the case. To do these things, you need to make an oral motion. Here are some examples:

- **Motion to Strike Testimony:** During the testimony of a witness, if the witness offers inadmissible or irrelevant testimony, you could make a motion to remove that testimony from the hearing transcript and to ask that the judge and jury to disregard that evidence. It is rare to need to make such a motion. Instead, if you are questioning the witness, I recommend politely interrupting the person and asking him or her to answer the question only. If you are listening to the witness, I recommend standing and advising the Court that you object to the testimony as inadmissible or irrelevant.

If you cannot remember or pronounce ancient Latin words such as "limine," don't panic, just tell the Court what you want to do. "Your Honour, I'd like to make a motion to exclude a portion of the letter the Plaintiff is seeking to introduce." Remember, a motion is just a request to the Court. If you make a clear, understandable request to the Court, that is better, in my opinion, than reciting Latin and confusing everyone except law professors.

- **Motion for continuance:** If you discover on the day of trial or a hearing that you need more time to prepare, you can ask the court to adjourn/continue the hearing to a new date. Some reasons might include:

  - The other side has not provided complete discovery to you yet and you are not sure what evidence they are going to rely on.

  - A surprise such as when the other side unexpectedly hands you a sheaf of papers you haven't seen before which they intend to use at trial.

  - A witness unexpectedly cannot come to court. (If the witness is properly subpoenaed but does not come to court, you may be able to ask the Court for a warrant for his or her arrest. You should carefully consider whether you will want a witness to testify for you if he or she is not doing so voluntarily.) A witness who receives a subpoena but has good reasons for not going to court should communicate with the Court rather than just deciding not to show up. He or she should consider whether there are grounds to make a Motion to Quash (cancel) the subpoena.

- **Motion for direction:** This is more a request to the Court for help with the way a trial or hearing is proceeding. Rather than guess what the next procedural step is or, worse, sitting down and doing nothing, politely tell the Court that you would like to ask for some direction at this point with respect to procedure, what is supposed to happen next.

9. Costs

The party who wins a motion hearing may ask the judge to order the other side to pay for costs (the expenses the party incurred to bring the motion). These typically include filing fees, photocopying expenses, and the cost for a lawyer.

Often judges will order "costs in the cause." This means that the party who eventually wins at trial will be owed costs by the other side. Because most cases do not end up going to trial (they settle), most litigants end up bearing their own costs for motions.

If you bring a frivolous motion or the Court determines that there is no reasonable basis for your motion, the Court may very well order costs against you and make you pay the other side's legal expenses. Motions that are intended to harass the other side or delay court proceedings may be found to be frivolous. The Court may even punish you by ordering punitive costs if your behaviour is truly over the line. This is a good reason to make sure that you only bring motions that are necessary.

10. What If the Other Side Ignores a Temporary Order? Contempt

A Court Order is really just a piece of paper telling someone what to do. If that person decides to ignore the order ("No, I won't pay," or "No, I won't drop the kids off for the weekend") but does not try to change the order by filing an appeal, what do you do?

To activate enforcement of a Court Order you will probably need to go back to court. Depending on your jurisdiction and the court, this may mean starting a new action or filing a motion. Typically, these are known as actions for contempt of court. See Chapter 12 for further discussion of contempt actions.

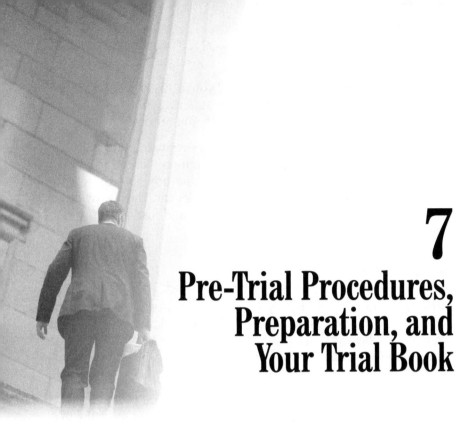

7

Pre-Trial Procedures, Preparation, and Your Trial Book

1. Stress Management

Lawsuits are my daily job. For a self-represented person, a lawsuit is on top of his or her regular job and can be an unfamiliar, baffling prospect. Plus, it is adversarial. So, if you're feeling overwhelmed and stressed, that's no surprise.

Before wading into the next round of trial preparation I recommend you take the time to do two things:

1. Do what you need to do to relax. For me, that's often going for a walk or a bike ride. Maybe for you it's watching a movie or taking a hot bath in the evening. Don't neglect the essentials: eating well and sleeping enough. Yes, preparing for a trial is time consuming. But you will not be as effective at getting ready if you're overwhelmed, sleep deprived, and suffering from heartburn.

2. Get a second opinion. By now, you're likely several months into your case. You probably are suffering from a case of seeing only trees instead of the forest. You need perspective.

Let me warn you about opinions from sympathetic friends and family. These are emotionally supportive, but they aren't legal opinions. The Court is going to take the facts that brought you to court and extract from them only what is legally relevant. The law will chew up and discard personal feelings of fairness and justice that are not legally relevant.

2. Jury Trials

The decision maker for a trial is either a judge or a jury. Most civil cases, however, are decided by a judge alone. If you want a jury to decide your case, you usually must request a trial by jury. (Jury trials are not available for some kinds of disputes. Check your Court Rules to see if a jury is available for your case.) If the other side requests a jury trial, you will likely have to have a trial by jury.

Even if you have a jury, a judge will still preside over the trial in order to decide how the case proceeds. Think of the judge as the master of ceremonies. He or she will decide who the guests are, what's on the jury's menu, and the order of proceedings. For example, the judge will decide what evidence is admissible and what is not. It is also the judge's job to help the jury understand the law. (The jury decides what the facts are.) Thus, even in a jury trial, the judge remains an important decision maker.

Generally, in my experience, a self-represented person is better off with a judge rather than a jury. Procedurally, not going with a jury means that you will not have to meet the deadline to request a trial by jury, you will not have to deposit any required jury fees, and you will not have to prepare instructions to a jury.

However, there may be advantages to having a jury. For example, if your case turns on easily understood law and you feel a jury will have more sympathy for your situation than a judge would, you may be better off with a jury. For example, in a personal injury case in which you slipped and fell at a business you may feel that a jury will have more sympathy for you than a judge.

A jury can affect the procedure of the trial (it may slow down the process) and that may have advantages and disadvantages, depending on your circumstances. Consider that with a judge trial, you only have to convince one person. With a jury trial, depending on the size of the jury, you will have to convince the majority of the 6 to 12 people.

Deciding whether to elect to have a jury is a complicated decision. If you are debating this, I recommend you consult with a lawyer and do further research on trials by jury. This book is written from the perspective of a judge-alone trial. My discussion of the jury trial process should be the beginning only of your research into proceeding with a jury trial.

3. Pre-Trial Hearings and Conferences

Before trial, there is usually at least one opportunity to go before a judge where the focus will be on getting ready for trial and whether settlement is possible. These hearings are usually very productive and help the Court to make sure that parties are both ready for court and that those cases that have settlement potential do not end up needlessly going to trial.

3.1 Settlement conference before a judge

In many jurisdictions, there is an opportunity to meet with a judge in a less formal hearing. These conferences have a variety of names such as, trial management conference or judicial case conference. For instance, for family law cases in British Columbia Supreme Court, these conferences are called Judicial Case Conferences (JCC). Because these conferences are meant to encourage the parties to have a frank discussion, you generally will not have the same judge at trial.

If the purpose of the conference is settlement, the judge should not make any orders that are not agreed to unless they relate to procedure. For example, if you and the other side discuss a settlement in which one of you will pay to remove a fence between your properties but do not reach agreement as to who will pay this cost, the judge should not make an order that you pay to remove the fence unless you both agree to this. It is important to ascertain at the beginning of the hearing whether the judge can make an order on an issue or not.

Procedural orders a judge might make at a settlement conference could be to set a deadline to complete discovery. For example, if you discuss when you will supply copies of your three most recent paystubs to the other side but do not reach agreement on this, a judge may have the power to make an order anyway. This is because the judge's job is to move the case along. Your Court Rules should specify what powers a judge has at a settlement hearing.

A benefit of these conferences is that a judge can make an order right at the hearing if you and the other side consent to it. This avoids having to bring a motion to court, scheduling that hearing, and appearing again in court. Another benefit of a settlement conference with a judge is that sometimes the judge is willing to offer a non-binding opinion on the case after hearing a summary of each side's evidence. This is not permitted in all jurisdictions and types of proceedings, however, and not all judges are willing to do this. If a judge does give an opinion, it can be a powerful incentive to motivate the parties to settle the case. If the opinion is not in your favour, you should carefully evaluate your case to see if there are ways to make it stronger before proceeding to trial.

What a settlement conference judge thinks based on a summary of the evidence may be different than what a trial judge or jury actually decides.

Here are some typical issues for consideration at a settlement conference with a judge:

1. Substantive issues about the case. For example, in a child support case, you and the other parties may agree on the amount of support.

2. Procedural issues:

   • Discovery deadlines: When will you exchange documents by?

   • Admissibility of evidence: Do you both agree that certain documents should be used at trial?

   • Timeline for motion hearings: What motions are upcoming and should some come first? Should some be scheduled together at the same time because they involve related issues?

   • Suitability of alternative dispute resolution such as mediation: Perhaps settlement potential seems good but cannot be completed at the meeting with a judge.

   • Suitability of expert reports: Does one party want to call an expert? For example, to appraise the value of property involved in the litigation. Does the other side agree to the expert or want a different expert?

   • Is a summary trial appropriate? This is a trial based on affidavit evidence and is suitable when there are not significant disagreements about the facts. It is not available in all jurisdictions and for all kinds of cases.

Settlement conferences with a judge vary widely, depending in large part on the style of the judge. I've been to settlement conferences where the judge has not used the courtroom, but sat down with the parties and lawyers at a round table. Here, the judge acted much like a mediator, and worked hard to make the parties feel at ease. He helped them to find common issues.

At another judge's conference, the judge held the conference in the courtroom and the hearing very much felt like a contested hearing. I, as one party's lawyer, described my position. Then the other side's lawyer described theirs. "Is there any possibility of settlement?" she then asked. The other side's lawyer said, "No." The judge nodded and the hearing ended.

In my experience, most judges will make a short speech on the importance of reaching settlement. You should be ready to briefly describe your position in less than a couple of minutes as well as what stage you are at in the litigation (e.g., whether discovery is complete, whether there are any upcoming motions).

Before consenting to any order, make sure you do not feel pressured. (**Tip:** Keep in mind or write out your absolute bottom line before the hearing so that you don't go below it. This bottom line is something that you should have carefully considered.) If you are feeling pressured by the judge or an aggressive lawyer on the other side to settle and are unsure whether the settlement deal is good or not, ask the judge for a break. Take a few minutes to think about the deal and remind yourself of what your bottom line was walking into the settlement conference. Are you below that line? Is there a good reason to be below the line such as something you are getting that you hadn't considered before? If not, you should probably walk back in and reject the offer.

If you are feeling pressured and the deal is not a good one, tell the judge that you can't accept the deal. There should not be any negative consequence to saying "no" at a settlement conference because in most jurisdictions you will have a different judge at your trial. If you are scheduled for trial with the same judge, consider filing a Motion to Disqualify that judge from your case on the basis that hearing the settlement conference has created a bias against you.

You can also tell the Court that you need time to think about any settlement terms.

3.2 Pre-trial conference and brief

Typically, before a trial the Court will want to gather information about the upcoming trial at a hearing, typically called a pre-trial conference. The court will ask questions such as: Is the trial still going ahead? How long will it be? Is there any chance of settling at least some issues? How many witnesses will there be?

Court Rules may require that the parties prepare a document called a pre-trial brief (or Pre-trial Memorandum) that asks and answers these kinds of questions. The pre-trial brief is served on the other side and filed in court. Be aware of filing deadlines for the brief.

In my experience the brief does not need to be agonized over. This process will help you get ready for trial and it may help you and the other side to settle some issues. If you find that some of the information in the brief changes (e.g., you need to add a new witness), you should let the other side know as soon as possible. You may need to file an amended brief if that is the case.

At the hearing the Court will be looking to evaluate three fundamental elements:

1. Are the parties ready for trial?

2. Is there a way to streamline the trial process? For example, by agreement on certain facts or issues.

3. Is there a way to wrap up the case without a trial? For example, by settlement or if a party has brought a Motion for Summary Judgment.

4. Trial Preparation

Go and watch one or two real trials, preferably the same kind you will have, before you have one. (No, not on TV!) Most trials are open to the public. Make sure it's a civil and not a criminal trial. Dress neatly, sit quietly and, if you want, take notes. The object to going to see a trial is to help you to feel comfortable in a courtroom. You can come and go as you please.

4.1 What you need to prove and how to prove it

Your legal research will have told you what you need to prove. For example, in many jurisdictions parenting custody disputes are about the "best interests" of the children. This involves a number of criteria (e.g., in BC you must consider "the child's emotional and physical well-being" as a factor in determining best interests). To do this, you can provide oral testimony that the child appears happy in your care. You can explain how your home is suited to the child (a bedroom, a yard, toys that the child likes to play with).

When I want to break down what I need to prove legally, I divide a page in two by drawing a line down the middle. On the left I write what I have to prove (e.g., emotional and physical well being) and on the right I list all the evidence that supports this. (For example, my client's testimony about the child and the space where he lives, maybe an expert report that has been obtained, maybe testimony from a teacher.)

This paper is the start of a checklist for the evidence you need to prove your case.

5. Your Trial Book: Get (and Stay) Organized!

There is a certain moment on a litigation file where it becomes clear to me that the case might not resolve itself before trial. Usually, that moment comes after there have been motions for temporary orders of some sort and after some form of settlement attempt (mediation, judicial case conference, or sitting down and talking). When that moment comes, I start a Trial Book. You should start one earlier than I do. Don't leave it until the trial is only a month away.

A Trial Book is separate from your legal file and from your book of pleadings. (Your legal file is where everything except your pleadings go: All your correspondence, all your notes, all your research. Your book of pleadings is everything that has been filed in court in chronological order.) Your Trial Book is a binder with everything you will need during the trial, in order. During the trial your Trial Book will be your main go-to resource. It is indispensable. It will give you confidence and make the trial go smoother. In my experience, preparation is the key to victory. (When I'm well-prepared, my chances of winning increase dramatically.)

5.1 How to make your Trial Book

Start your Trial Book by creating an index. Your index will essentially be a road map for what happens at the trial; each category (e.g., "Plaintiff's Statements") marks a distinct phase of the trial. You will consult your index and flip to each section of the binder as you reach that section during trial. Everything you need should be there, and if it's not, you should have further resources ready. For example, let's say the other side brings up a court rule with which you are not familiar.

You should have the rules of court printed (or borrowed from the library) ready so you can look up that rule.

Feel free to organize your Trial Book in a way that works for you. I like my Trial Book to be organized chronologically (from what happens first at trial to what happens last). I add a few extras, or things I might need at the end. I like to start with the pleadings; the meat in the middle is the legal argument, the witnesses, and evidence; and it ends with checklists so you can quickly flip to them to double check that you haven't missed anything. I also put copies of the checklists in the sections to which they pertain. (I don't want to ever forget to put something into evidence or make a critical point.)

Here is an index for a Trial Book. The tabs could be renumbered depending on how many witnesses you have:

Tab 1   Statement of Claim and Defence

Tab 2   Housekeeping, Pre-trial Matters

Tab 3   Plaintiff's Opening Statement

Tab 4   Defendant's Opening Statement

Tab 5   Plaintiff's 1st Witness [add name]

Tab 6   Plaintiff's 2nd Witness [add name]

Tab 7   Plaintiff's Exhibits

Tab 8   Plaintiff's Closing Remarks

Tab 9   Defendant's 1st Witness [add name]

Tab 10   Defendant's 2nd Witness [add name]

Tab 11   Defendant's Exhibits

Tab 12   Defendant's Closing Remarks

Tab 13   Statutes and Laws

Tab 14   Case Law

Tab 15   Pleadings for Trial (I only add pleadings into the binder if they are ones I will be referring to or putting to a witness and in the pleadings binder.)

Tab 16   Checklists

Tab 17   Exhibit Numbers

Tab 18   Other Documents Needed for Trial

5.1a   Tab 1: Statement of Claim and Defence

I like the Statement of Claim and Defence to go right up front because they offer a frame of the issues. This is important: Only what is in the Statement of Claim, Defence, and any Counterclaims will be a substantive issue during the trial. If something is not included here, and you think it should be, you may need to file an amended Statement of Claim, Defence, or Counterclaim. There are strict deadlines for these, so consult your Court Rules.

If any doubt is expressed by the judge about a particular issue being within the scope of issues before the Court, I can turn to my claims tab and say, "Yes, that issue relates to this claim right here." Also, if the other side starts to raise something not within the scope of the pleadings, I can object and point that out to the judge.

5.1b   Tab 2: Housekeeping, pre-trial matters

Before the trial actually begins, the Court may want to check with you and the other side on a number of issues affecting how the trial is going to proceed. There issues are generally informally referred to as housekeeping issues.

Is there anything that you wish to bring up before the trial begins and evidence starts being admitted? Will there be any motions before the trial such as a Motion to Exclude Evidence (if you think the other side is going to try to introduce inappropriate evidence)? If so, advise the Court.

Has there been any agreement on any facts? If so, advise the Court so that these facts can be admitted as proven.

Be ready for questions: Who are your witnesses? Are they present? (They should be if you are the plaintiff. If you are the defendant and it is a multiple day trial, and you are sure that they will not be needed until another day, they may not need to be present on the first day. However, it is better to be safe than sorry. I always try to have all my witnesses present on the first day just in case the case settles in the hallway on most issues and my witnesses are needed for the remaining issues.) How long do you expect each of your witnesses to testify? Witnesses should be asked to wait in the hall until other witnesses finish testifying (this is known as "sequestering"), then they may sit in on the hearing if they wish.

If a witness is not available for the full trial, you should bring the Court's attention to this and request that the witness be allowed to testify at a time that he or she is available. (If the witness is only available by phone, you should file a written motion well in advance of the trial and with proper notice to the other side, requesting that he or she testify by phone.)

If you are presenting any audio recordings or evidence that requires any set-up, advise the Court. (Ideally, you should speak to the court registry ahead of time to ensure that any equipment you need is already in the courtroom.)

5.1c Tabs 3 and 4: Opening statements

Have your opening statement written out. Take notes on the other side's opening statement so you can understand the other side's case and make sure your case addresses the issues raised. Also, you will want to see whether as the trial progresses the other side manages to prove what they claim they will prove in their opening. If they don't, be sure to tell the Court that when you make your closing remarks. See Chapter 8 for how to write your opening statement.

5.1d Tabs 5, 6, 9, and 10: Witness Tabs

Use a tab for each witness you will introduce and each witness the other side will introduce. For your witnesses, have your questions for direct examination written out. As I will explain in Chapter 9, I also write down my cross-examination questions for the other side's witnesses.

I divide a page into two sides. On the left I write the question. Underneath I write the answer and information I am seeking. The right side of the page is blank. This is where I will write in the witness' actual answers.

I also list the evidence I want to get in through that witness. For example, I will write, "Put contract dated March 14, 20XX, to witness."

Have blank paper in each section for notes when the other side cross examines your witness and to compose any redirect questions.

5.1e Tabs 7 and 11: Exhibits

This tab should be used if you do *not* have a book of documents, which is the best way to handle documentary evidence in a trial. (See Chapter 10.)

You cannot simply show a judge a document and expect it will become evidence in your trial. It first has to be introduced into evidence. This is usually done by a witness identifying the document during examination. That witness can be you if you are testifying. (For example, "Your Honour, this is a letter dated March 28, 20XX, sent by the Defendant to me.")

Any document that you wish to introduce into evidence goes into the tab for your role: either plaintiff or defendant's exhibits. You should have the original for presenting to the Court, a copy for the other side (although it will have been disclosed earlier), a copy for the judge, and an extra copy just in case. (If you are having a jury trial, with the judge's permission you may be able to provide a copy to each juror.) I put each document and its copies in a plastic three-hole-punched sleeve. If, however, your documents are too extensive and you do not have a book of documents, you may need a separate file folder (or box with dividers) for your documents. If you have separate file folders, have an index to those folders in this tab. For example, Folder #1, Letter to me from defendant dated March 31, 20XX.

For the other side's exhibits, you may not know which documents they will introduce. This is a place to put the documents which you expect the other side to use. Alternately, you may have to bring all documents the other side has disclosed to you, organized as best you can.

5.1f   Tab 8: Closing remarks

Keep blank paper behind this tab. You will not be able to write your complete closing remarks before trial because you don't know exactly what will happen as the evidence is presented and witnesses are subject to examination. However, as you get closer to the trial date read Chapter 11 on closing arguments and wrapping up. In this tab, you can sketch out some of the agreed-upon facts, what you anticipate the evidence will be, and the law. I recommend writing:

1. The law you want the court to know about.

2. How you anticipate the law will apply to the evidence. (This is the part you will have to adapt and change, thinking on your feet or during a break, to how the evidence actually is at trial.)

3. How any cases you've found in your legal research are relevant and helpful.

4. A list of what you are asking for and why it is your position that you should get these things.

5.1g Tab 13: Statutes and laws

When I refer to a particular statute, I like to have a copy ready to hand to the judge, particularly if I'm focusing on the interpretation of that law. I tell the judge that I have a copy if he or she would like to have one. Oftentimes, the judge appreciates this. Have enough copies for the other side and the clerk, too.

5.1h Tab 14: Case law

It is generally expected that you will provide copies of any cases you will use to the other side before the trial. There may be a court rule in your jurisdiction requiring you to do so. During the trial, you will hand copies to the judge and to the other side if they require a copy. Don't worry if you do not have cases! You may not need case law. You will have to assess whether you need them (because the facts and law are complicated) or do not (the law clearly applies to the facts) as you do your legal research.

5.1i Tab 15: Pleadings

You will have your Statement of Claim, Defence, and any Counter-claims at Tab 1. These are probably all you will need. (Any motions are a thing of the past now unless they relate to procedure or evidence at trial. What happened at a motion hearing for a temporary order should make no difference to your trial judge.) I only add pleadings into the binder here if they are ones I think I might be referring to or asking a witness about.

5.1j Tab 16: Checklists

This tab is optional because although you should have checklists you may find it easier to put them in different sections (e.g., a checklist of evidence to elicit from a witness can go in that witness' tab).

5.1k Tab 18: Other

There may be other categories you will want to add to your Trial Book. For example, you may want to add a tab for expert reports, or if you are in a family law case about support, you could have a tab for financial statements.

6. Your Book of Exhibits

Some jurisdictions require or allow the filing of a Book of Exhibits. This is an indexed, spiral-bound book of copies of any exhibit you intend to introduce into evidence. If this is required or allowed in your jurisdiction and if your trial involves lots of documents (more than 25 let's say), being able to put them together in a book will be a Godsend for the smooth presentation of your case. Your jurisdiction may also call for a Joint Book of Exhibits. That means that you and the other side must agree on which documents go into the joint book. If you cannot agree, you will have to introduce those other documents one by one at trial or you can create a separate book for your own documents. It would also be helpful if you have a Joint Book of Exhibits to have a short agreement specifying what you have agreed to about the documents. Terms you may wish to include:

- The documents are true copies of the originals.

- The signatures and dates on the documents are accurate and as indicated.

- Postmark, email, and fax dates are as indicated.

- Mailed, faxed, and emailed documents were received.

Whether you use a filed Book of Exhibits or simply have the documents loose (in a file folder to organize them), it is important to have your documents organized as soon as you can.

7. Other Pre-trial Preparation

If your trial is two months away, you should have already assembled and done the following:

- Listed all necessary facts to prove each element of your case and how you will prove each fact.

- Collected names, addresses, and phone numbers for all your witnesses. Make sure they are available for all trial days. Issue subpoenas if necessary.

- Interviewed witnesses and taken notes. Make sure you have obtained from your witnesses any documents in their possession that are relevant.

- Made sure you have disclosed all evidence that is relevant per Court Rules, taking care not to mark or alter original documents, and that expert reports are complete and conform to any Court Rules.

- Reviewed Court Rules carefully, checked limitation dates, and put all dates where something needs to be done in your calendar.

- Developed a theory of the other side's case. Reread any affidavits the other side has filed and looked over their pleadings. It may help if you take a piece of paper and list all the facts the other side must prove or disprove and look at how they will do this (i.e., what evidence do they need? How will they attack your evidence?). Next, figure out how you will refute their position.

Part Two
The Trial and Beyond

8
Trial Day Proceedings

1. Typical Order of Trial Proceedings

Typically, a trial proceeds in this order:

1. Pre-trial matters such as motions and discussions about how the trial is going to be conducted.

2. Plaintiff's opening statement.

3. Defendant's opening statement: Sometimes this can come after the plaintiff closes his or her case.

4. Plaintiff's witnesses: The plaintiff will question a witness and then the defendant may cross-examine that witness.

5. Plaintiff's closing argument (this may come now or after the defendant finishes presenting his or her case).

6. Defendant's witnesses. The defendant will examine a witness and then the plaintiff may cross-examine that witness.

7. Defendant's closing argument.

8. Judgement.

If you have a jury, jury selection would take place before #2, the Plaintiff's opening statement. After closing arguments, there would be jury instructions from the judge and then jury deliberation before #8, the judgement. The way I've set out the order can be changed by a judge.

Sometimes exhaustion and time limitations do not permit the level of preparation I talk about. The minimum you need to do is put time into thinking about what each phase of the trial will involve.

2. Before You Leave Home

On the morning of your trial, there isn't time for any more preparation, but you do have time to make sure you are dressed appropriately. Wear conservative clothes that will show the Court that you take this matter seriously.

Bring snacks for the morning break and afternoon break. Trials are exhausting and you will need to keep your mental focus.

3. Default Judgement

What happens if the other side fails to show up in court? If you are the plaintiff, you can ask the Court to enter a default judgement against the other side. A default judgement means that your claims, as long as the judge finds the Court has the jurisdiction to allow them, will be allowed and you will win your case. For example, if you claimed $50,000 in damages, the Court could order the other party to pay that amount. You will need to prove to the Court that the other side was properly served.

If you are the defendant and the plaintiff fails to show up, you can ask the judge to dismiss the plaintiff's case. If you have counterclaims, you can ask the Court to enter a default judgement on your counterclaims. You will likely need to prove to the Court that you served the counterclaims on the plaintiff.

Default judgements are more easily overturned than a judgement made after a full trial. If a default judgement has been made against you and you disagree with it, you should immediately find out what you need to do to set that judgement aside. Often the deadlines to do so are very short. If there are compelling reasons for not appearing in court (e.g., you were hospitalized), courts often will set aside a default judgement as long as the request (usually made by a motion) is made as soon as possible.

The lesson here is that you should always show up to court. Even if you know you're going to lose, don't miss the opportunity to show up and become a human face so that the judge will think twice before approving all the relief the other side has asked for. You might lose but still be able to reduce the amount of legal fees the other side wants, for example.

4. Your Job at Trial

If you are the plaintiff, your job is to prove the claims in your Statement of Claim by at least a balance of probabilities. This can also be called a preponderance of the evidence, and is generally the standard of proof in civil matters. It means that the claims you allege are more likely than not to be true. Some civil actions require a higher burden of proof; this higher standard is usually less than the criminal standard of a reasonable doubt but higher than a balance of probabilities. It means you will have to have even stronger evidence. Check your jurisdiction and Court Rules to determine the standard for your case.

If you are the defendant, your job is to make sure that each of the elements in the plaintiff's claims are not proven on a balance of probabilities. You will want to introduce enough doubt into the judge's (or jury's) mind that the claims were more likely to have *not* occurred. You will want to either create doubt about the plaintiff's facts by attacking the facts or offering your own facts that tell a different story which contradicts the plaintiff's facts.

4.1 Thoughts on demeanour

When in court, observe the rules:

- Stand when the judge enters.

- Stand when you are addressing the court.

There are also ways to influence the goodwill of the judge:

- Don't argue with the other side.

- Never interrupt the judge when he or she is speaking.

- Always address your remarks to the court. Don't make nonverbal commentary while the other side is speaking such as rolling your eyes, sighing, gasping, etc.

- Don't interrupt when the other side is speaking during their opening, closing, or housekeeping part of the trial. However, if what the other side says is outrageous or offensive and you feel you need to interrupt, stand up. The judge will know that you want to say something. If that doesn't work, politely say "Your Honour, may I respond," and wait for the judge to give you that opportunity. (Of course, you should stand and interrupt by saying "objection" if there is some valid reason to object such as, during the other side's testimony if they are providing hearsay testimony.)

5. The Trial

Arrive 30 minutes early at the courthouse; take 15 minutes to set up and 15 minutes in case something goes wrong. Scout out parking at the courthouse ahead of time; bring a friend to help you carry your materials. Find the list of all the cases that day to see what courtroom and judge you've been assigned.

Check in by introducing yourself to the judge's clerk (he or she might be at the desk in front of the judge's desk), and wait in your courtroom. The clerk will call the case. The judge will ask if you are ready to proceed. At this point, flag any procedural issues for the judge (e.g., if a witness isn't available until the afternoon, let the judge know).

When you unpack, the first thing you'll want to lay out is your Trial Book. Stack your evidence in a manner that is easy to access.

5.1 Witnesses

Before a witness testifies, he or she should not be present in the courtroom to hear other evidence. Ask your witnesses to wait in the hall. This is so that his or her testimony is not influenced by other evidence during the trial. If the other side's witnesses are present in the courtroom, let the judge know.

Your witnesses will probably be nervous about testifying. Before court, put them at ease; tell them that it will be you asking them questions first, that your examination will be just like a conversation with you, and remind them that you've gone over the questions with them already (you should have). On cross-examination, remind them of your witness preparation (listen to the question, only answer the question, and relax). Tell them that if they get flustered or upset, they can ask the judge for a break. (It will be up to the judge to decide if they get one, of course.)

5.2 Opening statement

The purpose of an opening statement is to orient the Court as to what the legal dispute is about and what you think should happen. It is also your opportunity to show the Court that you can be trusted, that you are prepared and that you are the better guide through the dispute than the other side.

Opening statements are not evidence. Never assume that what you say in an opening statement will become part of the evidence. For example, if you tell the Court in your opening statement that you witnessed the defendant striking your child, you will still have to testify to this event when you are on the witness stand.

Do not tell the Court you will prove something that you turn out later to be unable to prove or that is inadmissible. Make sure any evidence you refer to is going to come in. (If you have uncertain evidence, wait until your closing to summarize it.)

If you can, let your opening statement tell a story: Who you are, why you're in court, and what you want.

Your opening statement is your chance to provide a succinct summary of why you are in court, what the evidence will show, and what the outcome should be. Only, you might not get a chance to make an opening statement. In my experience, if a trial is a day or less and there is no jury, your judge might simply ask the plaintiff, "Is your first witness ready?" Don't be alarmed: You have two options if this happens. You can request that you be permitted to make an opening statement or you can go along with the judge's direction and bring out your first witness. If you want to request that you be allowed to make an opening statement, explain why this will help the Court; however, in my experience, you should do so only if you believe that strategically there is a good reason to provide the Court with an opening statement. A good reason may be that the facts are confusing and a brief summary will help the Court understand the testimony and evidence as it unfolds.

If the court does not directly tell you not to make one, I recommend you do make a brief opening statement. I lean towards brief because I want the evidence to make the impression and, if my case is strong (and it should be if you're pushing forward with a trial), the facts will speak for themselves and be more effective directly from a witness. At this point in the trial, the judge may or may not have read the pleadings. (Never ask the judge if he or she has read the pleadings.) The judge may have heard a motion or done your pre-trial. Whether the judge is familiar with your case or not will influence how long your opening statement should be. However, it is difficult to know how familiar the judge is. Generally, I begin with all the basic information. If the judge has reviewed the pleadings, he or she will generally indicate to me (either verbally or by body language) that I should move things along.

If you have a jury trial, an opening statement is even more important. Unlike a judge, jurors are not used to the courtroom process and the way information is elicited. An overview of your case may resonate with a jury in a way it wouldn't with a judge. (Judges are skeptical and know that an opening statement will be crafted in a way that might not be totally in line with the way the evidence actually comes out.) For a jury trial, a clear, positive opening statement can make your case.

Your opening statement should not be argumentative. Save that for your closing. Do not try to impress with legal jargon or how much research is on your side. In the midst of hearing oral testimony, this is what you hope the judge or jury will look back on to help him or her sort through confusing and conflicting evidence to begin to piece together the version of events that he or she will rely on when making a decision.

Your opening statement should be written ahead of time. However, when you show up in court I suggest using bullet points of the information you need to explain so that you don't sound stilted reading out loud. Also, the judge might interrupt you and you may have to ad lib your opening to accommodate the judge's questions and the judge's style.

If you are a defendant, you often will have the choice of making your opening statement after the plaintiff's opening statement or after the plaintiff has finished presenting evidence and his or her case is closed. Which is better?

1. After the plaintiff's opening statement: The advantage here is that before the judge has even heard a word from the plaintiff's witnesses, you can begin sowing the seeds of doubt. However, you won't have to wait too long to do this because you will be able to cross-examine the plaintiff's witnesses as soon as the plaintiff finishes direct examination. Also, sometimes when the plaintiff's case isn't that strong, it's better to let him or her shoot himself or herself in the foot rather than do it for the person.

2. At the beginning of your case: The advantage of making an opening statement after the plaintiff's case has closed is that you can incorporate what happened during the plaintiff's presentation and your cross-examination of his or her witnesses. You can make your opening responsive to the plaintiff's actual case as presented in court.

If in doubt and your judge gives you a choice, consider making your opening statement right away after the plaintiff's opening statement so that the seeds of doubt are sown early.

If you are the plaintiff drafting an opening statement:

1. Explain who you are. Explain who the other side is.

2. Tell the Court briefly what your claims are.

3. Summarize how you are going to prove your claims. For example, if you need to prove that a fence is built on your property and not on your neighbour's (and thus you have a right to an injunction preventing your neighbour from tearing it down), you might explain that you are going to call a surveyor as a witness.

4. Anticipate and respond to the defendant's defences.

5. If the defendant has counterclaims, explain how you respond to them.

6. Sum up what you will prove and what you want the Court to do.

If you are the defendant drafting an opening statement:

1. Tell the Court who you are.

2. Tell the Court what your defences are and summarize how you will disprove the plaintiff's claims. Note that you will not have to disprove a claim if the plaintiff failed to prove it in the first place. For example, if the plaintiff in a boundary dispute about a fence failed to provide evidence that the fence was on his or her property, you might choose not to provide any evidence that it was in fact on your property.

3. Explain what your counterclaims, if any, are, and summarize how you will prove them.

4. Summarize the facts and explain to the Court what you want it to do.

See the download kit for sample opening statements for a defendant and a plaintiff.

5.3 Trial Book and notes

The opening statement part of your Trial Book should have a copy of your statement. You will need paper and space to take notes about the other side's opening.

As a defendant, you may need to adapt your opening after hearing the other side's opening. For example, in a contract dispute case, if the plaintiff's opening surprisingly talks about introducing evidence that you lost custody of your children in another proceeding, you will want to tell the Court that what did or did not happen in a family law proceeding is irrelevant to the proceeding at hand. Your statement should have the main points highlighted and allow for space to add in new elements.

If you are the plaintiff, you should take notes of the defendant's opening for several reasons. First, you want to understand what the defendant is trying to prove and to disprove. Is the opening what you expected or are there unexpected curveballs? When you are giving your closing argument, address whether the defendant has succeeded or not in proving or disproving the points she said she would in her opening. As well, the defendant's opening statement may give you a heads-up about areas you will need to attack in your cross-examination of the defendant's witnesses.

9
Witnesses

A witness at a trial is someone who provides evidence that helps you (or the other side) prove or disprove one or more claims in the case. Usually, the testimony is oral and he or she is sworn in so that it is under oath.

If you are the party asking (or calling) the witness to testify, you will ask the witness questions. There is a specific order and strategy to how you present these questions and elicit a witness' testimony. If you are a party and wish to testify, you will simply tell the Court what your evidence is after you have been placed under oath.

Evidence rules for your jurisdiction will contain specific information about whether evidence you obtain from your witnesses is admissible.

1. Subpoenaing Witnesses

A subpoena is a written notice requiring a witness' attendance at Court. Consult your local Court Rules to learn how a subpoena is issued and properly served on a witness and how much lead time is required. You could also be required to pay a witness a small fee for attending court.

It is a good idea to issue and serve all your witnesses with a subpoena rather than rely on them to show up out of the goodness of their hearts. If witnesses are subpoenaed and they do not show up for court, they may be subject to arrest.

In cases where a witness is unable to attend court (e.g., due to illness) you may need to show the Court that you subpoenaed that witness if you want to ask for the hearing to be adjourned (continued) to a new date.

As a general rule, I always ask a potential witness if he or she is willing to testify before serving him or her with a subpoena. A cooperative, friendly witness is helpful whereas an uncooperative, hostile witness may hurt your case. I also make sure I interview all witnesses ahead of time to make sure the evidence they have is helpful. Call a potential witness, explain the reason you might need him or her to testify, and ask for a meeting to go over what he or she knows. Take notes.

A subpoena can require a witness to bring documents or other evidence with him or her to court. This is known as a subpoena *duces tecum*.

2. Direct Examination

Asking a witness you have called to the witness stand is called "direct examination" or "examination-in-chief." After you finish direct examination of your witness, the other side will then be able to cross-examine your witness. How a witness is questioned in direct and cross-examination is different and there are specific rules you must follow.

Direct examination is your chance to prove your case. This is the way you prove, if you are the plaintiff, each element of your case. If you are the defendant, this is your opportunity to disprove the other side's facts or offer a different version of events.

The plaintiff can choose which witness to question first. The defendant, when he or she begins, will also have a choice of the order in which he or she wishes his or her witnesses to testify. Generally, the best way to proceed is chronologically.

A witness (or you if you're testifying) must have firsthand knowledge of the event about which you are asking/telling. For example, if your witness heard from a friend that your car was involved in an accident, that is not firsthand knowledge. The witness must have seen the accident.

The key element to examining a witness during direct examination is that you cannot ask a question which suggests an answer (a leading question). A helpful way to think of a leading question is a question that can be answered with "Yes" or "No." (For example, "You washed the store floor, didn't you?" is a leading question. Some other examples are: "The fence was white, wasn't it?" "Isn't it true that you did not put a warning sign on the wet floor?" These questions contain an answer and require a "Yes" or "No" response.) Instead, questions should start off open-ended so that the witness, not the questioner, will supply all the information. The best way to conduct direct examination is to let the witness tell the story as much as possible, with your guidance to move him or her forward to talk about the right subject matter. Short, open-ended questions are best, such as:

- Can you describe the fence?

- What happened when you arrived at home on July 10, 20XX?

- What happened next?

- Can you tell us the condition of the floor?

These questions often ask who, what, when, and where. Consider the following open-ended questions:

- Can you tell the Court who was driving?

- Can you tell the Court what happened?

- Can you tell the Court where you were on Monday, May 3, 20XX?

To follow up on open-ended questions, you can ask for specific information. For example, "What colour was the fence?" "What time did you wash the store floor?" "Which aisles did you wash?" These questions ask for specific information. They are not leading, because they do not imply an answer one way or another. If you cannot get the information you need with an open-ended question, requests for specific information are your next best tool on direct examination.

Your questions should be as short and direct as possible. You want the Court to focus on the witness, not you, at this point in the proceeding. Also, make sure you don't offer any commentary on what the witness says.

When it is time to present your evidence (see Chapter 8 for trial order), tell the Court who your first witness is. The judge will ask that he or she come in (from the hallway, where he or she has been waiting so as to not overhear others' testimony), and will likely direct him or her to be seated in the witness box. In terms of where you should stand or whether you should sit, different courts and different judges have different styles. Hopefully you will have seen a trial in the courthouse previously; if not, your choice is usually to stand with your notes at a podium or to remain standing at counsel's table, when it is your turn to speak.

Do not stay seated unless the Court invites you to do so. If you are unable to remain standing, advise the Court that you have to sit for medical reasons. Have your Trial Book open to your examination questions and have any documents to show the witness is ready. Speak clearly and slowly and look at your witness when you ask a question. Looking at a witness will help him or her focus on what you are saying. It will also improve your performance. If your head is down and you are simply reading questions, it will appear that you are not interested in the witness' testimony, an example you do not want the judge (and jury) to follow.

Also contained in the idea that the questions not supply information to the witness, is the requirement that you establish a foundation for each topic of questioning. A helpful way to think of this is to imagine you are building a story from scratch. As you add any new information the source of that information *must* come from the witness. So, if you ask a witness, "When did you observe that the fence was removed?," you have to first have the witness testify about all the information that is contained in that question. You will have to first get the person to testify that he or she observed a fence before he or she observed that it wasn't there. Here's an example of how to do that:

Plaintiff: Can you tell the Court where you live?

Witness: I live at 32 Crescent St, in Mayville.

Plaintiff: And how long have you lived there?

Witness: For about eight years.

Plaintiff : And what can you observe across the street from your house?

Witness : There are two houses.

Plaintiff: And within the last week have you observed anything between the two houses?

Witness: Well, there's a garage and part of a fence there.

Plaintiff: If we go back about six months, can you tell me what you observed with respect to this area between the houses?

Witness: Well, there was a new and complete fence and it stretched from the garage to the street.

Plaintiff: And today, what would you observe with respect to that fence?

Witness: Today the fence is partly gone. Now, it starts at the garage but ends about ten feet from the garage.

Plaintiff: So can you tell the Court when this change from complete to part of a fence occurred?

These questions situate the witness as the source of the information. The witness saw the fence and has personal knowledge of it. A person who only heard about the fence or read about it in the newspaper would not be a good witness as he or she is not the direct source of the information.

A good way to think of direct examination is to imagine that you have an empty table. This is the starting point for the examination and where evidence will go. Next you ask a question. When the witness answers that question she provides information (or evidence) that can go on that table. Now you have some information on the table. Think of that information as a building block; as you compose your next question, you can use that piece of information in the question. But you yourself, the questioner, can never put information on the table. For example:

Question: Can you tell us about what happened on May 3, 20XX?

Answer: That's the day I drove to work and hit a deer.

Question: Can you tell us how you hit the deer?

If the questioning began by asking how the witness hit a deer, we're making the assumption that he did in fact hit a deer. The questioner is supplying that piece of information, not the witness. The Court needs the witness to say this, because only what the witness says, not the questions posed to the witness, are evidence. So, I first need to establish that a deer was hit and then I can begin asking questions about how the deer was hit.

Now that you know you cannot ask leading questions on direct examination, it's time to learn the exceptions. In the following instances, you can ask leading questions:

1. Preliminary matters: To move things along, the Court will usually permit leading questions at the beginning of a witness' testimony to establish who the witness is. Generally, you should establish the witness' name, address, and some broad connection to the proceeding such as place of employment (if it is relevant) or relation to the parties (e.g., your spouse or other family member). Here's an example:

Examiner: Can you tell the Court your name please.

Witness: Lucy Luckless

Examiner: And you reside at 123 Main St, Victoria, BC?

Witness: Yes.

Examiner: And you are employed by County Fence Supply in Victoria, BC?

Witness: Yes.

2. Uncontested evidence: Like preliminary matters, if facts are not in dispute, the Court will generally permit leading questions about information you and the other side agree on to move things along. For example, if you and the other side agree that your witness was standing at the south corner of Main and Hastings on July 2, 20XX, at 10:30 a.m. but disagree on what the witness saw, you could ask:

Question: Is it correct that on July 2, 20XX, at approximately noon you were standing on the south corner of Main and Hastings? (This is a leading question.)

Answer: Yes

Question: (The next question should not be leading.) Can you tell me what you observed at that time?

3. Helping the witness: You may need to set up a question by referring back to previous testimony. This may be important if the court has taken a break. For example, if your witness testified the previous day that he did not observe brake lights on the plaintiff's vehicle before a car accident, you could ask him, "Now, you testified yesterday that you did not observe brake lights on the plaintiff's vehicle, correct?" You could follow up with a relevant question. "Can you tell the Court about when you noticed the brake lights come on?"

4. If you know that a witness you are going to call is opposed to your position (e.g., you call the other side as a witness), you may ask the Court to declare her a hostile witness (also known as an "adverse witness"). If the Court grants your request, you will be permitted to cross-examine the witness. In other words, you will be allowed to ask questions that have a "yes" or "no" answer. You can still ask a hostile witness open-ended questions, however if she is hostile she will be unlikely to provide the comprehensive, narrative-style answer to open-ended questions that will be helpful. In other words, she won't cooperate.

   You may find that someone you at first thought would be cooperative and answer your direct examination questions is proving to be difficult. He may give terse answers or even ask you questions. Don't answer! You aren't testifying. He might embellish his answers with testimony that helps the other side, not you. The judge may have to warn him to cooperate. (You can ask the judge to tell the witness to answer the questions you are asking.) If your examination is being frustrated by the witness' lack of cooperation, you can ask that the judge declare him a hostile witness, in which case you will be allowed to ask leading questions.

When you are done examining, thank the witness and tell the judge that those are all your questions for this witness. You may have a chance to ask more questions for issues that arise on cross-examination.

2.1 Improper leading questions on direct examination

If the other side objects to a leading question you asked on direct examination, and if the judge sustains the objection (agrees with the reasons for the objection), the witness will not have to answer the question. Generally, you will be given a chance to recompose and put a new version of the question to the witness.

If the other side doesn't object to your improper leading question, you may have still hurt your case. You have not properly brought forward evidence by laying a foundation for it. In other words, your evidence might be missing information. Further, all testimony is transcribed in case there is an appeal; if you did not obtain clear evidence and statements from the witness, those will not be in evidence for any appeal.

See the download kit for a quiz about direct examination questions.

Tips for Examining Your Witnesses

1. Keep the examination as short as possible while eliciting all the necessary information.

2. End on a high note.

3. Be sympathetic to your witness. He or she will feel nervous. Convey a friendly, sympathetic attitude; imply that you are indeed a friend. You might be the only familiar face in the room. Put him or her at ease by acting relaxed (even if you aren't!).

4. Aim for specificity. If you cannot obtain an exact date, try to get as close to one as possible. For example, month and year is okay and season and year is better than nothing. Have the witness provide first and last names of anyone mentioned.

5. Ask factual questions and not for the witness' opinion.

2.2 Witness preparation

Witness preparation is a means for you to know what to expect of a witness on the witness stand, a way to help you and your witness feel comfortable with each other, and to allow for the smooth flow of your direct examination. I usually prep a witness after I have conducted at least one thorough interview with him or her. I meet with the witness in person and go over my drafted direct examination questions. This helps both of us feel comfortable, and ensures the witness understands the questions.

Importantly, it serves as a way to confirm that the witness will answer with the testimony you expect! (The other side can ask your witness if you prepped them. This shouldn't make a difference in the case as lawyers always prep witnesses.)

It is important to tell your witness to answer the questions honestly; explain to the witness that a deliberate lie could, depending on your jurisdiction, have possible criminal consequences, and does more harm than good. If your witness is found to not be credible, this will cast a pall on your whole case. If you think your witness is not going to be honest (or for some reason appears dishonest), thank her for her time but consider not calling her at trial as a witness.

Another consideration during this stage is to ask yourself if the witness will make a good impression on the judge (and/or jury).

Next, you will want to cross-examine your witness, to prepare her for cross-examination by the other side. This preparation will help you to anticipate some of the weaker points about your witness's testimony. In this regard, you might want to ask questions about these weaker areas in direct examination in order to steal the other side's thunder.

Remind your witnesses:

1. Dress neatly.

2. Be polite.

3. Answer questions either by looking at you or at the judge (or jury).

4. Only answer the question asked.

5. Speak clearly. Nonverbal answers such as head nodding are not useful because they do not appear on a transcript or recording. (If your witness does nod or says, "mm hmm" in court, simply ask if he meant "yes" or "no" with respect to your question, or ask him to explain what he meant.)

6. Answers should be as specific as possible.

7. Refer to people mentioned during the examination by first and last name.

8. If the witness doesn't understand a question, she should say so and ask the questioner to repeat the question.

2.3 You forgot a question?

Let's say you've finished your direct examination of your chief witness, the other side has cross-examined him, you've each had a brief opportunity for redirect and re-cross (explained below), but after the witness has been excused by the judge, you remember a key question and information you completely overlooked. What do you do?

Well, you may be out of luck; that is why you making a bullet-point checklist of the evidence you need from each witness is essential. However, you can ask the judge, and it may be in the judge's discretion to allow you to recall your witness. In my experience, you probably will not be allowed to recall your witness. If, however, you realize you've forgotten a line of questioning and the witness is still on the stand (let's say she is being cross-examined), when that is finished, you may ask the judge to allow you to reopen direct examination on a new line of questions. Again, it will be entirely up to the judge to decide. However, if the witness is still on the stand, your chances are better.

2.4 The witness can't remember something

Even though you've gone over your questions with the witness and he has provided an answer to a specific question in the past, when he is on the witness stand, it is possible that the witness will blank, or misremember or can't remember a date or the name of an important person in the case. If that happens and a document will help the witness' memory, consider showing that document to the witness. Remember though, that anything you show to the witness you also have to show to the other side and to the judge. That means, whatever information is on the document may be used by the other side. (Note that you will have probably already disclosed to the other side all documents that are relevant to the proceedings according to your jurisdiction's disclosure rules. However, the judge will not have seen these documents unless they were introduced into evidence at an earlier stage of the trial.)

Here's an example of how refreshing the witness' memory might look at trial. Note that rules of evidence are complicated on this issue (e.g., you may or may not wish to have the document you are showing to the witness introduced as evidence) and you should review the law in your jurisdiction if you anticipate having to refresh a witness' memory:

Plaintiff: Can you tell the Court what the weather was like when the accident happened?

Witness: Uh. I can't remember.

Plaintiff: Did you know that information previously?

Witness: Yes, but I can't remember now.

Plaintiff: Your Honour, I'd like to show the witness the accident report she signed and submitted to the insurance company in order to refresh the witness's memory.

Judge: OK. This will be Exhibit #1.

Plaintiff: [After passing a copy of the document to the witness, as well as copies to the judge and the other side, and giving the witness a moment to review it.] Do you recognize this document?

Witness: Yes, it is the accident report I had to fill out for the insurance company.

Plaintiff: And is that your signature on page two?

Witness: Yes.

Plaintiff: Can you now recall what the weather was like on the day of the accident?

Plaintiff: Yes, it was raining.

2.5 Testifying yourself

Often in cases where a party is self-represented, he or she is the main witness. Unlike cases where a party is represented, a self-represented person will have to tell the story without the prompting of questions. (After you are done, the other side will ask you questions in cross-examination.) The judge may ask you questions during your testimony. Once you've answered and if the judge appears to have no further questions, you should continue to testify.

Stick to the evidence that supports your claims (or disproves the plaintiff's if you are the defendant). Direct examination is not the time to make an argument. That comes later. Keep it brief, to the point, honest, and as much like a story (i.e., as interesting) as possible.

Can you read out a statement? That is up to the judge in your case. Generally, if you do have a written document you wish to read from, you will have to give a copy to the other side and to the judge. This might give the other side a slight advantage in cross-examining you as they will have a checklist of information that you have testified to and will be looking for even the very slightest deviation between what is written down and what you say. Reading, also, can sound stilted and less genuine than being able to look the judge (and/or jury members) in the eye and tell your story. It is not as effective in my experience. Instead, if you are nervous, have a checklist prepared, or notes. If you need to look at the checklist or notes, tell the judge that you would like to have permission to review your notes. While this is generally permissible, the other side may request a copy of anything you look at while testifying, so be very careful that that document only contains information that will not hurt your case or embarrass you. (If your nickname for the other side is less than flattering in your notes and you need to use those notes when testifying, change them!)

As part of your opening statement, tell the Court that you will be testifying. You can choose the order in which to present your witnesses. Note that an interesting advantage of going last is that you will have heard the testimony of your other witnesses so you can fill in any holes they left. (All other witnesses are expected to not be present in court during the trial before they testify; parties, however, are allowed to be present.) However, going first is a good way to give an overview of the case and is often a good way to make a positive first impression. Don't get lost in the middle. As a lawyer, I usually like my client to go first.

The judge may ask you to take a seat in the witness box (a box with a seat in it usually to the right or left of the judge) or will allow you to remain at the table in front of him or her (counsel's table). The judge's clerk will then administer an oath that you are telling the truth. If you wish to introduce evidence (e.g., documents) after you've laid a foundation for the document, hand a copy to the judge's clerk (not directly to the judge unless he or she wishes) and one to the other side. Mark down the exhibit number for the document.

3. Cross-examination

Cross-examination is a way of asking questions of a witness, to test or challenge the evidence presented on direct examination. It is also a means to test the reliability and credibility of witnesses. Are the witnesses honest? Do they have a reliable memory?

Once the other side has concluded direct examination, you will have an opportunity to cross-examine the other side's witnesses. There is no requirement that you ask questions. In fact, you should not cross-examine a witness if you believe the evidence he or she has provided is the truth, is reliable, and there is no further information that you could elicit that would help your case.

Cross-examination is generally not as important as direct examination. Further, because you are dealing with a hostile witness (the other side's witness) and have not had an opportunity to prepare with the person, her answers are going to be, to a certain extent, unpredictable. This isn't the part of the trial you can easily control.

The truthfulness of the witness (credibility) is always at issue. Using the previous example, if you raise the issue of the defendant's business assets to show that he is cheating on tax returns, that is permissible because it relates to honesty (i.e., his credibility).

It's an old legal truism that there is "no property in a witness." That means that either party can contact a potential witness for the other side before trial and interview him or her. I always try to do this; sometimes the witness will refuse to speak to me because he or she knows I'm the other side's lawyer, and that is his or her right. (You may be able to question him or her at an examination for discovery if the Court Rules for your jurisdiction allow this.) Sometimes the witness will speak to me and, if that is the case, I generally tread lightly, asking open-ended questions and being as polite as possible. If there are some challenging questions I want to ask, I save them until the end of the interview in case he or she hangs up.

3.1 Why cross-examine?

There are two main benefits to cross-examination:

1. The witness answers the way you want. Maybe he provides helpful information or discredits himself.

2. By posing leading questions, even if the witness does not answer the way you want, you are suggesting a different version of events from what the witness has offered. Showing the court that you challenge the stated version of events can be very powerful.

There are times when you are going to be better off not cross-examine a witness. For example, if you do not dispute the witness' testimony, then you probably will not have any questions. Or there might be circumstances where cross-examining a witness may make you look bad. For example, if in a parenting time dispute, the defendant's mother testified about how wonderful the defendant is as a parent, it is pretty obvious that this witness is going to be biased toward her daughter. There might be little gained by asking her general questions such as "Isn't it true that the defendant is not as attentive to the children as she could be?" Grandma is going to back up her daughter and you will likely look overly aggressive if you challenge a witness toward whom a judge (and jury) will likely feel sympathy. If anything, you could ask her a couple of very specific questions. For example,

"During the visit on March 18, 20XX, isn't it true that the plaintiff dropped the children off at your home with dirty diapers?"

3.2 How do you cross-examine?

Cross-examination questions are largely leading. The witness usually has little choice but to respond with a "yes" or "no" answer. For example, "You stabbed Desdemona, didn't you?" is a leading question. The only answers are either, "yes" or "no." One reason you will want to use leading questions is to prevent the witness from simply retelling the evidence that he gave under direct examination. You don't want this because that evidence was probably unfavourable to you. On cross, you can hone in on the details that you want to pin down.

Some lawyers say you should never write out your cross-examination questions ahead of time. This is because cross-examination should rise out of what happened on direct examination. Thus, because you haven't listened to direct examination yet, you can't know what questions to ask. I write out my cross-examination questions and know many excellent lawyers who do the same. Guessing at what you'll need to ask will help you to be ready for what actually happens. It also gets me thinking about the case generally and can help me bolster and strengthen elements of my case.

It is usually best to start off cross-examination with questions that are easier for you to ask and the witness to answer. In other words, don't start off aggressively. If you've got some real zingers or want to impeach the witness, save that for the second half or towards the end; at the beginning, you likely will want the witness to cooperate, and begin to trust you a little, not keep up her guard.

Remember that the judge (and jury) are always watching you and the way you treat a witness will leave an impression. Don't shout and don't lose your temper. Be cool and reasonable (don't be cross on cross). If you are impolite, the judge may remonstrate with you, which will not help your case. Abandon the TV images of a swaggering, disgusted lawyer laying in to a witness who breaks down and admits his lies. That isn't the way it typically happens.

As with direct examination, you will either remain at counsel's table or stand at a podium. You should not approach the witness or pace. You can use the witness to introduce documents or to cross-examine her with respect to already introduced documents.

3.2a What if the witness won't answer with a "yes" or "no"?

Usually on cross you want to avoid the longer answers that direct examination creates. For example:

Defendant: You didn't do a shoulder check before you turned right on Main Street, isn't that right?

Witness: I was going less than 50 km/h which is well under the speed limit and driving with extreme caution, as I always do. In 30 years, I've never even had a parking ticket.

Try interrupting (as politely as possible):

Defendant: You didn't do a shoulder check before you turned right on Main Street, isn't that right?

Witness: I was going less than 50 km/h.

Defendant: [interrupting] But the question is whether you did a shoulder check or not. I put it that you did not do a shoulder check, isn't that right?

Witness: Yes.

If that doesn't work and the witness continues to evade your questions or provide longwinded answers that repeat what he said in direct examination, you can ask the judge to direct the witness to answer the specific question.

Sometimes it can be important to use cross-examination in a way that brings forward evidence that doesn't attack the witness or try to unpeel some layer of deception. Consider a family law case in which much of your cross-examination is attacking the witnesses' ability to parent. For example, you've asked questions like, "You've never changed Kimberly's diaper, have you?" and "You never picked up your daughter from school, isn't that right?" and "Last Christmas, you didn't show up for Kimberly's school play, isn't that right?"

Because parenting time is at issue, you can ask positive questions as well such as, "The plaintiff always changed Kimberly's daughter, isn't that right?" and "The plaintiff has always been there after school to pick Kimberly up, hasn't she?" and "The plaintiff attended Kimberly's school play last Christmas, didn't she?"

Thus, cross-examination can be used not just for tearing down but also for building up. Combining the two approaches can be very effective.

During any break of the trial (e.g., for lunch), you should generally not communicate with any witness still being examined about his or her testimony.

4. Impeaching

Impeaching a witness means that you have called that witness' credibility into question. There are often specific Court Rules about how to do this. Impeachment can cast a witness' entire testimony into doubt because it makes her look dishonest or unreliable. When you are prepping your witnesses for direct examination, you will want her to review previous sworn evidence such as affidavits and depositions so that she doesn't inadvertently testify differently at trial and thus create an opportunity to be impeached.

Impeaching a witness is simply done by asking a question that raises doubt about the witness' honesty. Common sense and reason will be your guiding principles in cross-examination. It is not necessary to memorize any specific formula to impeach a witness. Though there are different ways to create doubt about honesty (prior inconsistent statement, bias, a history of criminal convictions), impeachment is less a technique than common sense.

Note that if the impeachment is not about a material fact, it will not have as much impact as impeaching a witness on a less important fact.

An easy way to impeach someone is to show that what he is saying in court is different than what he's said before (preferably also under oath). The process goes something like this:

Defendant: You testified in direct examination that you observed a rabbit in your garden on March 12, 20XX, isn't that right?

Witness: Yes.

Defendant: Your Honour may I show the witness a copy of his statement from June 3, 20XX?

Judge: Yes.

Defendant [To witness]: Please turn to page 22 and read out line 44.

Witness: (reading) I might have seen a rabbit or it could have been a squirrel on March 12, 20XX. I'm not sure.

Defendant: So, today you are sure that it is a rabbit but at the examination you weren't sure?

Witness: I guess I'm not sure.

This is known as a "prior inconsistent statement."

If a witness on your side is impeached, you may be able to do some repair work. Maybe there is a good explanation for the inconsistency (the witness saw a documentary on rabbits after the examination for discovery, so his squirrel/rabbit ID skills have improved). If so, you can have him provide that explanation on redirect examination. Remember that you cannot communicate with the witness who is still under oath during the break.

5. Objections

When the other side is asking questions (or wants to introduce a document) in a way that is unfair, you can tell the Court that you object. It will be up for the judge to decide if he or she agrees with your objection. The judge may say that your objection is "sustained" meaning the witness does not have to answer the question. If the judge says "overruled," then the witness will have to answer the question. Frequently, when a judge agrees with an objection, the party who posed the improper question will have a chance to rephrase the question so that it is fair.

There are complicated rules about what questions are objectionable. To try a case and be ready to object, a lawyer will have been trained on and reviewed the applicable Rules of Court, practice manuals, and case law. During civil trials that involve self-represented persons, however, spotting improper questions is often a matter of common sense.

You can also object to statements made in the other side's opening or closing statements. It is rare to do this. However, if the other side is misstating evidence, you should stand up and object. For example, if at trial a witness testified that the defendant was paid $15,500 for a renovation job, but the plaintiff states in her closing that the amount the witness testified to was $50,000, you could object.

Be firm when you make an objection but try not to speak at the same time as the other side, the judge, or a witness. Instead, use the act of standing or raising a hand to get the judge's attention. If that doesn't work, say "Your Honour" or "objection." Do not argue with the judge if your objection is not sustained. (If the judge made a mistake, that might be an issue on an appeal.)

5.1 Objections to questions

Some common objections:

- Leading question: Generally these are not allowed on direct examination. They are permitted on cross.

- Confusing question: Sometimes, the questioner will try to set up a question by providing background information. In doing so it may become unclear as to what the questioner is actually asking.

- Vague question: A vague question does not clearly identify the information it seeks. (This is more of an issue on cross-examination.)

- Compound question: Sometimes the questioner will ask more than one question at once. "So, the car went through a red light and then hit the bicycle, correct?" The questioner simply needs to break this down into two questions. "The car went through a red light, correct?" and, if the answer is yes, "After going through a red light, the car hit a bicycle, isn't that right?" (If the answer was "no" then the follow-up questions might be about the colour of the light; "But the light was yellow before the car entered the intersection, wasn't it?" and then move on to ask about the car hitting the bicycle, "After entering the intersection, the car hit a bicycle, didn't it?")

- Question about confidential or privileged material: For example, if the question asks whether a party offered money for a settlement, that is confidential; if it is about a visit to the party's lawyer's office and what the party and the lawyer discussed, that is privileged.

- "Asked and answered" question: If the questioner repeats questions he or she has asked before.

- Misquoting of prior testimony: On cross-examination the questioner may misquote the witnesses' testimony on direct examination. For example, if the witness testified that a car was going

40 km/h but the questioner asks, "You testified today that the car was travelling 45 km/h, didn't you?"

- The questioner is argumentative: This happens when the questions are meant only to antagonize the witness. For example, "Do you know what perjury is?" or "Why are you telling these lies?" or "I can't believe anything you are saying."

- When a question asks what another person is thinking: It is not possible to know what another person is thinking so a question such as "Why do you think he did it?" is asking a witness to guess, which isn't admissible evidence.

- The questioner doesn't lay a foundation for the question: For example, "How many eggs in the frying pan were burnt?" First, the questioner needed to establish that there were eggs in the frying pan.

5.1a How to object to questions

When the question (or statement in a party's opening or closing) is made, you should immediately stand while saying to the judge (not the other side), "Your Honour, objection" or simply "objection." When you have the judge's attention, state as succinctly as possible the basis for your objection. For example, "the question is confusing," or "the question asks for hearsay evidence," or "the question is irrelevant." Don't worry if you don't remember the exact name or type of objection. Just explain to the judge why you think the question is unfair.

If the witness has started to answer the question, and the judge has sustained your objection, you can ask the judge to "strike" the witness's testimony with respect to the improper question. This means that that testimony will not be part of the official record of the hearing. This may be important if there is an appeal because appeals are usually based on the hearing record.

5.2 Objections to testimony

If you wish to object to the testimony of a witness (rather than the question of a party or lawyer), the act of standing up will usually signal to the judge that you object. Once the witness pauses, tell the judge that you object and give a quick, one word if possible explanation (e.g., "hearsay"). Here is an example:

Lawyer: Please tell the Court what happened after the car entered the intersection?

Witness: Well, Mr. McGregor told me there were no brake lights on ... [Witness pauses for a moment.]

You: [standing] Your Honour, objection. Hearsay.

5.2a Common objections to testimony

Common testimony objections:

- **Irrelevant:** The testimony is not relevant to the material issues in the case.

- **Hearsay:** The testimony offers secondhand information.

- **Opinion:** The testimony doesn't talk about facts, instead offers an opinion or a guess.

- **Legal conclusion:** An example, "I think the plaintiff was negligent." The conclusion is for the judge (or jury) to make, not the witness.

5.3 What to do when the other side objects

If the other side objects, first let the judge listen to the explanation of the objection. Most often there will not be any reason for you to say anything unless the judge looks at you and asks for a response. If you disagree with the basis for the objection, explain to the judge why you think the question or testimony objected to is appropriate. If you have posed a question to a witness and the judge sustains the objection, you will not be able to ask that question. Think about a way that you can redo the question so that the basis of the objection is dealt with. Short questions are always a good idea. For a confusing question, make the question simpler. For a compound question (two or more questions in one), break down the question. If the objection was because you didn't lay a foundation, ask yourself how you got to the question and back up, so that you establish the building blocks for the question. If you are completely stymied and cannot think of a way to repose the question, tell the judge. Though the judge cannot advocate for your side, if you're lucky, he or she might offer procedural guidance. Don't try to be a lawyer, but do the best job you can and let the judge know when you're in trouble. (Even lawyers do this. We're all human.)

6. Incriminating Testimony

If you are concerned that you will incriminate yourself by your testimony, you should talk to a lawyer before you testify in court. The same advice applies if your witness is concerned that he will incriminate himself by his testimony, he should talk to a lawyer before he testifies in court. Sub-section 5(2) of the *Canada Evidence Act* and, for example, s. 4 of the *BC Evidence Act* provides that when a witness testifies to something that tends to incriminate him that evidence will not be admissible in any subsequent proceedings. This is also guaranteed by Section 13 of the Canadian Charter of Rights and Freedoms. The only exception to this protection is where the evidence presented leads to a prosecution for perjury.

7. The Expert Witness

An expert witness can do something other witnesses cannot do: He or she can provide an opinion. For example, an expert can tell the Court that, in his expert opinion, the value of a home is $1,000,000. Or, that the plaintiff's parenting is detrimental to a child. (Depending on your jurisdiction, experts may be able to offer other testimony that doesn't follow the usual evidence rules.)

Your first question is whether you need an expert. This will likely require some legal research. When you read cases with similar facts to your own, were expert witnesses used? The next question is whether the judge (or jury) can get the same information that the expert can provide without an expert. For example, if the issue is the value of a business, is there some way to establish the value without an expert? The average judge, juror, or even business owner cannot usually establish the value of a business. (Do not assume the judge is an expert. He or she is not.)

However, if the issue is bad parenting, the average judge, juror, or parent usually can evaluate evidence about parenting and make a determination about bad parenting. The third question is whether you can afford any fee the expert may charge; experts typically charge a fee whether for written reports or to appear in court.

Whether to hire an expert is often a very difficult decision. Where possible, ask the other side if they will agree to hire an expert together with you. (Sometimes certain jurisdictions even require this.) The risk here is that you will get a bad report which the other side will now possess; if you select the right expert, however, the risk may be worth it.

With respect to finding an expert, you may want to consult with a lawyer for a brief amount of time to talk about what experts he or she recommends, or to get his or her opinion on an expert that the other side has proposed as a joint expert. If you are unable to get legal assistance on evaluating or finding an expert, I recommend you —

1. do some research, obtain CVs and any other information available on the web; and

2. phone potential experts and interview them. Ask the person what his process is, what his fee is, and what experience he has had with similar cases.

An important element about hiring an expert is to know what she is being hired for. For example, if you hire an expert to value your business, be clear about whether you are talking about market value or something different. If you are hiring an expert in a child custody matter, be clear as to what issues she is to look at. Is she going to interview the children? Is she going to make recommendations for a parenting schedule? Make sure it is set out in writing.

Your Court Rules may have certain requirements about how to call an expert witness to testify during a trial or to submit an expert report into evidence. It is essential that you check those rules. There are often strict timelines for when an expert report must be completed in order to be admissible at trial.

7.1 Expert testimony

During your trial, you must persuade the Court to accept that your expert is in fact an expert in his subject area. The other side may argue that your expert isn't qualified to provide the information you want him to provide. Thus, a mini-hearing (known as a "voir dire") will occur to determine if the witness should be qualified as an expert in your trial. In this mini-hearing, your examination will first address the witness' credentials. What experience and/or education qualify the witness to be an expert? (This will depend on the kind of expert you call.) You will likely need him to bring a copy of his résumé for the Court (and the other side). The other side may wish to cross-examine the expert with respect to his qualifications and this may occur before he actually testifies about the matters at issue in the case. The judge will decide if the expert is qualified or not.

Experts can offer testimony that other witnesses cannot. If you are opposed to an expert, you will need to research the scope of what exactly the expert can and cannot testify to. You can challenge the expert's credentials, the basis for her opinion, or call your own expert witness to rebut the other side's expert's evidence.

If you have agreed on an expert with the other side (a joint expert) but do not agree with the opinion, you can examine him on the witness stand to challenge his opinion, or call your own expert witness to contradict his opinion.

10
Exhibits

1. Getting in Your Evidence

Unless you and the other side have agreed that a piece of evidence is admissible, documents and other physical evidence (e.g., a photograph or a recording of a voicemail) are typically introduced into evidence during a trial by presenting that piece of evidence to a witness (or you, if you're testifying) who is able to identify it for the Court. It is then up to the judge to decide whether that evidence is admissible or not. Once it is admissible, the evidence becomes known as an "exhibit" and an identification number is assigned to it.

The trial system is built on the idea that everything needs to be tested to see if it is fair and reliable. If you simply showed up with a document, let's say a contract that you will pay Lucy Luckless $7,000 to paint your home, and asked the judge to admit that contract into evidence, the judge will be suspicious. Are the signatures real? How does the judge know it's not something you drafted and faked a signature? The way to persuade a judge that the evidence is reliable is to have a witness who is familiar with the document identify it under oath. Establishing that reliability is known as building a foundation for the exhibit.

There are strict evidence rules about what foundation is required for each kind of exhibit. I recommend that you read the rules of court for your jurisdiction so that you know how to introduce a document or other tangible evidence to trial. There are many nuances that this book does not deal with for reasons of conciseness and brevity. Frankly, in many proceedings you will not need to know the detailed requirements to build a foundation for certain pieces of evidence. A custody proceeding, for example, or a case in small claims court, will not usually require a detailed knowledge of evidence law. Even a divorce that involves real estate and a dispute about the defendant's self-employment income may not involve strict application by the judge of these requirements. What may happen is that a judge will be liberal with admitting evidence but will give the evidence that doesn't look as reliable less weight (less importance) when he or she makes a decision.

Exhibits must, like all evidence, be relevant to a claim or a defence (or a witness's credibility). Showing up with your child's favourite stuffy because you think it might elicit sympathy from the judge in your custody case isn't going to fly. Your exhibits should either help your claim in some way or help to defend you from the other side's claims.

Here's an example of how entering a document (in this case, a contract which helpfully has signatures on it) into evidence may look:

Party: Your Honour, I'd like to show Ms. Luckless a document.

Judge: That's fine.

Party: [Handing a copy of the contract to the other side and a copy, or if required, the original, to the judge, then a copy to the witness.] I am handing you a five-page document. Do you recognize this document? [The purpose of this question is to establish that the witness has seen the document before.]

Witness: Yes.

Party: Would you please tell the Court what it is?

Party: It's the contract I made with Mr. Ames.

Party: And is there a date on it?

Witness: Yes July 7, 20XX.

Party: And is that your signature on page five?

Witness: Yes.

Party: And is there another signature on page five beside yours?

Witness: Yes, it's Mr. Ames' signature.

Party: How do you know that?

Witness: I watched him sign it.

Party: And is this document the same as when you signed it?

Witness: Yes.

Party: Your Honour, I'd like to introduce this document into evidence.

Judge: Any objections?

Other side: No.

Judge: OK, this will be Exhibit One.

Party: Thank you, your Honour.

You can then proceed to examine the witness on the document. You can also refer to it (including what it says) in your closing. The other side can also use this document during the trial now that it is admitted as evidence. Of course, the other side may have objected to the document and, if the judge sustained the objection, that would mean you could not use that document.

What happens if the witness cannot identify a document? Ask the judge to mark the exhibit for identification only. That way, the document will be given an exhibit number. You can still ask the witness questions about the document but you will not be able to rely on the contents of the document (what it says) in your closing argument unless you are able to have another witness provide a sufficient foundation (i.e., have another witness identify it and provide enough information about it so that the judge feels it is reliable and admits it).

If you are testifying and representing yourself, introducing a document may look something like this:

Party: Ms. Luckless and I signed a contract together. Your Honour, I'd like to introduce the contract document into evidence.

Judge: Please describe the document.

Party: [Retrieving the contract and handing a copy to the judge and a copy to the other side.] Your Honour, this document is dated July 7, 20XX. It is a contract between Ms. Luckless and myself. On page five, it has my signature.

Beside my signature is Ms. Luckless's signature which I know is her signature because I watched her sign the document. The contract looks the same as the day both Ms. Luckless and I signed it.

Judge: Alright, that will be Exhibit One.

Party: Thank you, Your Honour.

If you are having a jury trial, the next step is to show or read out the document to the jury. You should ask the judge's permission before doing this.

What if part of a exhibit is unreliable but the rest is okay? For example, an email that contains hearsay statements by another person, but the rest of contains helpful information that it reliable; a judge may admit only part of that email.

2. Focusing on Documents

Whether you (as a witness) introduce the document or your witness introduces it, you do not need to read out the whole document. You can proceed to use a document admitted into evidence to question the witness or use it in your testimony. For example, if a clause of the contract says that a $5,000 deposit is due by a certain date, you can ask the witness whether that was paid. Or you can explain that yourself during your testimony. (There are exceptions and limitations to this. For example, if a document contains hearsay statements, you may object to them being relied on for the truth of their contents.) Sometimes it can be effective for a witness to read out a critical part of the document.

2.1 Expert reports

An expert report is a document that you may ask the judge to introduce as an exhibit. If the parties cannot agree that the report should be admitted (see section 5. for exhibits by agreement), the party introducing the report will need to provide a foundation for the expert by providing his or her qualifications and will likely need to have the expert present in court to establish sthat the report was indeed made by him or her and to give the other side an opportunity to examine the expert on his or her qualifications as an expert, and if the report is admitted into evidence, on the content of the report. If you don't like an expert report, you should consider questioning the expert and having your own expert testify or provide a report.

3. Photographs, Voicemails, etc.

The most common form of exhibit is a document. For example, a contract, a sales receipt, a bank statement, or a cheque. However an exhibit can include any tangible object that a judge admits into evidence. In other words, things. The most common exhibits that I've seen in civil trial other than written documents are photographs. As well, I've seen audio recordings (e.g., a voicemail message) admitted.

The list of possible things that could be introduced at trial is probably endless. I've seen things as strange as a whole door (in an assault case in which the door was damaged) actually be taken in and out of a courtroom as an exhibit.

Non-document exhibits must be introduced into evidence in a similar way as a document. You must establish a foundation. It is beyond the scope of this book to explain all the rules for each type of exhibit; the underlying principle, however, is that the witness must have some relation to the object and must be able to provide information to the Court that suggests that the exhibit is reliable. For example, if it is a photograph of a vehicle introduced to show damage to a vehicle, the witness must have seen the car in real life so as to be able to identify it in the photograph.

Here are examples of common exhibits:

- **Photographs:** Information that will help photos be admitted includes that the witness can identify what the picture shows (e.g., "That is my car," "That is the intersection at Pembroke and Fernwood," or "That is Lucy Luckless"); the witness is familiar with what the photo shows at time of the photo (e.g., "That's my car right after the accident," or "that is my house before I built a fence"); and that the photograph is accurate (the photograph fairly and accurately shows the intersection of Pembroke Street and Fernwood Avenue).

- **Sound or video recordings:** Sound or video recordings can be tricky to introduce at trial. A judge may have questions about whether the recorder (camera, cell phone) was in good working order, whether it is capable of accurate recording, whether what the operator (who should be the witness) also heard or saw the event as it was recorded, and proof that the recording was not tampered with. The most important element is that the witness recognizes the voices or images of persons on the recording. You will need to have equipment ready to play the recording and made sure you have properly provided copies of the recordings to the other side.

- **Business records, government records, and bank records:** These come with some built-in safeguards so that the courts generally will admit them even if they contain hearsay, so long as a proper foundation is established. (For example, a bank statement might state that $1,000 was deposited on July 7, 20XX, into the defendant's account. Unless the clerk from the bank who made this deposit actually testifies that the money was deposited, then this statement is technically hearsay because the person who wrote it — said it — is probably not in court.)

  Business records are basically records created by an organization such as companies, community groups, or nonprofits in the ordinary course of their business. Examples include bills, log books, and letters. Government records may include police reports and health code reports. If you wish to rely on these documents, you must still establish a foundation for them. Frequently, you will have to subpoena to court the Keeper of the Records from the business. This is a representative from the business who can tell the Court that the records are indeed authentic.

  Be sure to research what foundation requirements are required for your jurisdiction. If you cannot do this research, remember the basic requirements for establishing a foundation: The witness is familiar with the document and can reliably talk about it. (In my experience in family and landlord tenant cases, the Court sometimes will not require a strictly by-the-book foundation for these kinds of records.) If you can offer testimony that corroborates the record, that will help strengthen the reliability of the record. (For example, let's say that I wish to introduce my bank statement to show that $1,000 was withdrawn from my account on July 7, 20XX. If I have already testified to this withdrawal by stating that I wrote a cheque for $1,000 and then describe what the statement is, that I've seen it before, that it was mailed to my address, which is printed on the first page, it is my experience that a court may not actually require a clerk from the bank to testify to establish foundation for this exhibit.)

- **Social media:** What if you want to introduce a tweet? Or a post from someone's Facebook account? A blog entry? This is an evolving area of law. It is important that you establish that the post is reliable. Can your witness assure the Court that the post is not from a fake account? Be sure that any social media evidence is relevant (e.g., to the other side's credibility) and not introduced simply to inflame or embarrass the other side.

4. Documents on Cross-Examination

You may need to ask an adverse witness (i.e., the other side's witness) questions about a document. In fact, documents can be very useful tools on cross-examination. Usually, you introduce documents through your own testimony or through your own witnesses. However, you may need to use the other side to introduce a document through their witness or when they are testifying.

5. Introducing Documents by Agreement

The ideal way to introduce a document into evidence is when the other side and you agree that it should be part of evidence. Judges are always relieved with this one less thing they have to do. For example, if you and the other side are in a contract dispute, you probably both will want to refer to the contract. Or in a family law dispute involving financial issues, joint tax returns may be important and necessary for both sides. Thus, you and the other side can agree that these documents will be introduced as exhibits. The easiest way to present and handle evidence is when it is bound in a book of documents.

The practical steps to reach an agreement are to first talk (phone) the other side and let them know what documents you think they also might agree to use as evidence. If a document will come into evidence anyway (i.e., there is no good reason not to admit it), it will make the objecting party look difficult and uncompromising. So, even if there is no advantage to agreeing to allow a document into evidence, simply showing the Court that you are willing to be cooperative and help move the trial along usually scores you a couple of points with the judge. (For a judge who has a busy schedule of hearings, making a trial move along in an efficient way is a top priority.)

Unless there are specific Court Rules about how to agree on documents to be introduced as exhibits, I recommend putting any agreement you reach with the other side into writing. Ideally, this would be a short contract. At the very least you should draft and send a short letter to the other side which states that you are confirming that you have reached an agreement that certain documents will be jointly admitted into evidence. You should list the documents in the letter (describing them in a way that includes their date). With any agreement on evidence, it will be up to the judge to make the final decision on whether the exhibits you have agreed upon admitting actually are admitted into evidence. You (or the other side) should tell the judge about their agreement at the very beginning of the trial when you are going over housekeeping matters. (Add this to your list of things to do in your Trial Book at the housekeeping stage.)

6. Strategizing with Your Witnesses about Exhibits

You will need to think about which witness (including yourself) is best suited to introduce each exhibit. Part of this process will mean that when you do your witness preparation, you should ask your witness the same kinds of questions that you will ask him or her at trial to lay a foundation (as covered in Chapter 9). For example, if you are in a slip and fall case and your witness is a family member who photographed the wet floor you slipped on, you will want to show the witness the photograph you intend to enter as an exhibit and ask him the foundational questions for a photograph: "Do you recognize what this photograph is showing? When was the photograph taken? Who took it?"

You may find that there is more than one witness who is familiar with an exhibit and can lay a foundation. You will have to think about the effect that each witness will produce. Does one witness appear more trustworthy than another? Choose your best witness to introduce evidence. You can always ask other witnesses questions about the same exhibit if that will advance your case.

7. Exhibit Organization

You're drowning in paper; you've got boxes of documents to introduce and only one trial day. What do you do?

You may have too many exhibits. Consider the following options:

1. Try to reach agreement with the other side about jointly entering exhibits: If you jointly agree on exhibits, you will not need to show them to a witness and lay a foundation for each exhibit. Instead, you will present the exhibits to the judge at the beginning of the trial. (Then, if you want to question a witness on one of them, you can but you may not have to lay a full foundation. You may still need to ask the witness questions such as if she is are familiar with the exhibit.)

2. Group exhibits together: For example, if you want to admit your bank statements from the last three years into evidence, instead of laying a foundation for each one lay a foundation

for them as a group. (Technically, a judge may say that a bank representative is needed to lay a foundation for bank records.)

3. Get rid of exhibits you do not absolutely need: Look at each of your claims and/or defences. Think about which exhibits best help your case. Ask whether the potential exhibits that aren't the best are necessary. Make a list of what is absolutely necessary and make sure you get those into evidence; if, as the trial proceeds, you need to dip into your backup documents, do so. But don't automatically try to introduce absolutely everything.

4. Organize: Once I've winnowed my exhibits down to the essential, there are two ways I organize exhibits for trial depending on how many I have. My organization is driven on the principle that I need to make everything as foolproof as possible. It is important that you use a method that works for you. If you are unable to quickly find a document during your trial, it may mean that you will not be able to use it.

   a) When I have fewer than five exhibits per witness, in my Trial Book, after my list of questions for the witness and after my blank sheets for notes and writing down new questions, I insert a plastic, three-hole punched sleeve. Into the sleeve I slip the exhibits I intend to introduce through that witness. I paper clip the four copies together. (One copy for the other side, one for the judge, one for the witness, and one for me.) If that sleeve won't hold all my exhibits for that witness, I move on to Option b, below. I usually write a simple description of what a document is on a Post-it note which I put on the first copy. For example, "Letter from me to Ms. Luckless, January 15, 20XX." I pull my exhibits out of this sleeve when that witness takes the witness stand.

   b) When I have more than five exhibits per witness, I put the exhibits into folders. I prefer to stack the folders in the order of my witnesses at the top of counsel's table. However, other people like to have them in boxes organized with proper hangers and tabs. Whatever method you use, make sure the folders are very clearly labelled. Because you might not actually put them to your witness in the order you expect, you should write out an index for the folder (inside cover of the folder works) and number each package of four copies of a document (use a Post-it note on the top of each document to describe it: Contract dated July 3, 20XX, and add an index number for yourself).

A Book of Exhibits is the ideal way to organize exhibits. Often this is either spiral bound or a binder and has page numbers. (A binder is useful when documents are not admissible because they may be removed.) This makes finding documents tremendously easy. Another tool from the discovery process may be a Book of Documents. This is a book of all the evidence you disclosed to the other side. I bring this with me to trial but never introduce it as an exhibit as it always has many more documents than I wish to introduce at trial. I like to have it (or a file box) of everything with me at trial just in case the trial takes a turn I didn't expect and suddenly I do need to fish out a document I didn't expect I'd need but now is important to my case.

Tip: If there are certain sections you want to draw the witnesses attention to, highlight those sections on your copy of the exhibit (not anyone else's).

8. Common Objections to Exhibits

Just as you can object to the testimony of a witness, so too can you object to whether a particular exhibit is admissible into evidence. If the judge agrees with the objection, the exhibit will not go into evidence and the judge (and jury) will not be able to rely on it to make a decision. If you have a jury trial, the judge may excuse the jury while hearing argument from both sides about whether the exhibit should be admitted, so the jury does not learn about the exhibit and end up relying on it if it is indeed excluded.

Here are some common objections to exhibits:

- **Relevance:** If an exhibit does not advance a claim or defence or relate to some issue at trial such as a witness' credibility, it can be objected to on the basis that it is not relevant.

- **Hearsay:** If the document reports another person's words and there is no exception to allow it, you can object to the document being admitted or object to the part of the document that is hearsay.

- **No foundation:** As discussed, the Court requires reassurance that a document is reliable, thus a foundation is needed. If you believe the other side has not provided a sufficient foundation, and you do not want a particular document to come into evidence, you can object. Often, failure to provide sufficient foundation is something that can be easily fixed by further questioning of the witness. Thus, you should really only object when you know that this document isn't reliable and should not come into evidence. You can also object if the foundation offered is, you believe, wrong. For example, if the other side is seeking to introduce a photo of your car alleging it was taken before an accident, and you know that it was taken after the accident. Even if the photo comes into evidence, you can still make that argument during the trial. For example, you can testify that the photo was taken after the accident and argue in your closing that the photo should be disregarded by the judge.

Here's an example of objecting to the foundation for an exhibit, where the foundation was questioned and the foundation was re-laid:

Party: Your Honour, I'd like to show Ms. Luckless a document.

Judge: That's fine.

Party: (Speaking to witness.) I am handing you a five-page document. Do you recognize this document?

Witness: Yes.

Party: Please tell the Court what it is.

Party: It's the letter I received from Mr. Ames.

Party: Your Honour, I'd like to introduce this document into evidence.

Judge: Any objections?

Other side: Yes. There is no proper foundation with respect to the reasons for the witness' belief that the letter is from Mr. Ames.

Judge: Sustained.

Party: May I reword my questions your Honour?

Judge: Go ahead.

Party: Have you seen this document before?

Witness: Yes. I received it in the mail around the beginning of October, 20XX.

Party: And is it in the same condition as that time?

Witness: Yes.

Party: Do you recognize the signature on page five of the document?

Witness: Yes, it is Mr. Ames' signature.

Party: And are you familiar with his signature?

Witness: Yes, I've received letters from him on many occasions. We have exchanged letters at least twice a year for the past ten years. That looks like his signature.

Party: I'd like to introduce this letter as evidence, your Honour.

Judge: It will be Exhibit 1.

Once the evidence has been admitted into evidence by the judge as above, the witness can be examined on it. You can also refer to it in your closing. The other side also can use this document during the trial now that it is admitted as evidence. Of course, if the judge sustained the objection, that would mean no one could use it.

- **Parole evidence rule:** It is unlikely that you will encounter or need to use this objection. (However, it is a term that is common in court so knowing it is a good idea.) When you have a written contract, any verbal statements surrounding the contract such as a promise not to perform some part of the contract or adding additional terms are generally inadmissible. However, verbal statements about a contract may be admissible in certain situations such as, when the contract is ambiguous.

- **Other objections:** Some of the objections covered in Chapter 9 about witnesses apply to evidence too. If you feel that a document is unreliable and that introducing it into evidence is unfair and will prejudice your case, I recommend that you consider objecting, even if you don't know the specific rule. That doesn't mean you should object because you don't like an exhibit or it hurts your case. Examples might include where an exhibit is a forgery, or the witness is unfamiliar with it (e.g., he is unsure what is shown in a photo), or it is not clear that the exhibit is what the witness says it is (e.g., she says it is a letter from a specific person but is unable to identify the signature or handwriting).

11
Closing Arguments and Wrapping Up

Even though it isn't mandatory, I always make a closing argument; even when I believe I've won the case and the judge is giving me a look that says, "OK, you've convinced me, let's go home," and the other side has started to pack up. I recap the favourable evidence, the law, and remind the Court what my client wants. Even if the judge is going to make a decision in my favour, I want the decision to be exactly what I want including being awarded costs. (It also creates a stronger record in case the other side appeals the case, or if my client and I decide we want to appeal.)

After the final witness has left the witness stand, the Court will often take a break before hearing closing arguments. This is your opportunity to pull out your draft written argument and the notes you've been taking during the trial, and bring them together.

1. What Is a Closing Argument?

Your closing argument is your last chance to communicate with the judge (and jury) to convince him or her that the facts and law support what you want to happen. Closing arguments can vary from just a couple of minutes to as long as an hour or more. You should aim to be as brief as possible. If a trial lasts a day, I usually aim to be done within 10 minutes to a maximum of 30 minutes. Even if the trial runs for several days, I still try to keep my argument as brief as possible, aiming for a maximum of 30 to 40 minutes. Often this works out to about 5 to 10 minutes of argument for every day of trial. Of course, if the law is very complicated and the evidence confusing, more time should be taken so that you can clearly lay out your argument for the judge (and jury). Pack the good stuff up front, before the judge begins to lose interest.

A closing argument typically consists of these elements:

1. A review and evaluation of the key evidence in the case: Highlight the facts. In other words, what happened at trial? What should the judge or jury take away from the admissible evidence? Did the facts support your claim? Explain why the facts did support your claim. (If you are the defendant, you'll want to explain why the facts do not support the plaintiff's claim and why the evidence supports your defences.) Talk about the credibility of the witnesses. Were your witnesses believable? Why? Talk about other evidence and whether it is reliable.

    Here's how the beginning of a closing argument might look:

    Your Honour, thank you for the opportunity to be heard today in Court. One year ago, I slipped and seriously injured myself at XYX Grocery because of their negligence in not placing a sign on the floor. The evidence you've heard today supports my claim that I deserve to receive compensation for the injuries I received that day. Let's look at that evidence ...

2. What the law says: Highlight the main building blocks of statute and case law that support your position.

3. Putting the law and facts together to reach a conclusion: For example, if the law says that parenting time must be in the best interests of the children, explain that and also that the evidence indicates that parenting time with you is in the best interests of the children (explain how); therefore, the children should have parenting time with you.

4. Telling the Court what you want: This is also known as asking for the "relief" you are seeking. Don't forget anything!

When it comes to quoting the law your job is to hone in on the elements that make your case and to distinguish (show as not applicable) the elements that might harm your case. Here's what I suggest you do: Focus first on the statutes, that is the laws and regulations, that apply. Try to write them in a way that starts at the beginning. Don't forget to include words in the definitions section of the applicable statutes. Courts and lawyers spend a considerable amount of time trying to understand what words mean. Those words are sometimes defined in the definitions section at the beginning of the statutes. Then get a pair a scissors and cut out each law and each definition. Next, imagine you have to explain the law to someone who is essentially from another planet (I mean the person has no understanding of the law). In what order would you explain the law to that person? Arrange your slips of paper in that order.

Next, take any cases your research has indicated to you are helpful. Write as briefly as you can the following:

- The name of the case.

- What the case was generally about in one sentence.

- What the case says that helps your case in one sentence.

Next, highlight any elements of the law or your cases summaries that you know or suspect that the other side will use for their case or interpret differently from you. These are the issues that will likely be where the fight occurs at trial.

Your next step is to take the work you've done above and prepare an outline of the law which you will put into your Trial Book. The law isn't going to change during the trial (okay, it's possible but very unlikely) so this is one outline that will not change much.

Your conclusion may be as simple as stating what it is you want. You've already set out the facts, and the law, now you're putting what the logical sum is of these two elements: What you want.

2. The Defendant's Closing

2.1 Part 1: The facts

Like a plaintiff's review of the facts, as a defendant you will describe the evidence that supports your defences. Just as important, you should highlight the elements of the plaintiff's claim that they have failed to prove. This failure might be due to weaknesses with the evidence. You should also point out what evidence is missing.

Here are some issues that you may want to raise:

- **Credibility:** Were the other side's witnesses believable? Let the Court know about any problems with credibility. You will also want to highlight the strengths of your evidence. For example, was one of your witnesses testimony corroborated by documents or another witness?

- **Reliability:** Was your evidence reliable? Was the other side's unreliable? Tell the Court how. If evidence was corroborated, that will help its reliability.

2.2 Part 2: The law

The plaintiff will have brought up the law that supports their position. Draw attention to those parts of the law that they brought up that are subject to interpretation or where the other side has neglected to mention or highlight those aspects of the law that are helpful to your defences and weaken their claims. For example, you may want to say something to the effect of: "Your Honour, the other side has raised the law surrounding best interests of the child. However, in doing so they did not mention that the child's views are part of this test. My understanding of the case law [cite any you have] is that the views of a child of our daughter's age, 14, should be given careful consideration by a court. The evidence before this Court was clear that the child's views were that she wanted to spend more parenting time with me."

Do you set out all of the facts and then all of the relevant laws? No. I proceed by issue. If the first issue is whether a contract was actually created, I will set out all the facts on that issue followed by the applicable law and then state my conclusion. Then I'll move on to the next issue, such as, was the contract breached? I'll set out the facts and laws on this and make a conclusion. If you go by issue, you will be telling more of a story. It will be more interesting.

You should refer to the burden of proof. This is critical if you have a jury trial. The burden of proof is just to what degree the plaintiff has to prove their case. In most civil (i.e., not criminal) trials it is usually a preponderance of the evidence. That means that the plaintiff must prove that their version of events is more likely than not to have occurred. As the defendant you will want to show how the plaintiff's evidence has fallen short of their burden of proof.

2.3 Part 3: The conclusion

Tell the Court what you want it to do: Dismiss the plaintiff's case and award costs against them. If you have counterclaims, remind the judge of exactly what you want him or her to order.

Do what feels natural for you to guide the judge (or jury) to the law, to the facts, and to your conclusions of what should happen.

3. Logistics: The Defendant Is Done so What Happens Next?

The person who made the first closing argument (usually this is the plaintiff) may be given a chance to respond to what the defendant said in their closing. This is called a "rebuttal argument." The Court will often also permit a very brief response by the defendant to the rebuttal.

A rebuttal, if permitted, is not an opportunity to have another kick at the can and repeat what you said in your closing. Rather, this is an opportunity to offer a response to any new issues that the other side has brought up. The idea is that because the defendant went second, they were able to respond to what you said so fair's fair, you should have a chance too. The Court will want you to keep a rebuttal very brief, a couple of minutes.

Let's think of an example: Let's say that you are the plaintiff in a child support case. You have offered evidence that the other side's income is higher than he claims in his Financial Statement and thus he should pay more support.

To your surprise, in the defendant's closing he argues that though his income is higher now, the evidence indicates that the average of his income, which is lower, should be what determines child support. Because you did not address the issue of averaging his income, you should ask the judge for an opportunity to respond to this as your rebuttal.

Rebut the rebuttal? Yes, the Court may allow the person who did not have a rebuttal to briefly respond to the rebuttal. However, this is usually up to the judge and he or she will want to shut down any back and forth arguing.

If the judge doesn't offer you a rebuttal, I usually only stand and ask to make a few more comments if there is some misstatement of important evidence or clearly incorrect statement of the law by the other side. I don't stand up if the other side merely interprets the evidence a different way (i.e., a way I don't like), or if they disagree with me on the meaning of the law. However, if they clearly get it wrong (e.g., they misquote a statute), I stand up and let the Court know. Heck, it's another point for my side (as long as I don't look like I'm overreacting) and it might be the last word in the trial (so make it a good one). Or, if the other side overreaches, let them have the last word and leave that as their last impression.

4. The Judge during Closing

If the judge is trying to move the trial along, he or she can cut you off to ask a question, prevent repetition, focus you on the relevant issues, or otherwise manage the fair and expeditious flow of a trial. What a judge should not do is absolutely deny your right to be heard. (Denial of a right to be heard may breach a judge's professional code of conduct.) That right is not unlimited and that is why a judge will steer you away from the following:

- Repeating yourself.

- Making irrelevant arguments.

- Arguing undisputed issues.

- Attacking the other side unnecessarily and making irrelevant personal comments.

- Offering your opinion. For example, "In my opinion, I should get custody of my daughter." Instead, you want to say, "The evidence supports my claim that it is in the child's best interest to live with me."

- Referring to evidence not admitted to trial: Your best piece of evidence may not have been allowed into evidence by the judge. If it is not admitted, you cannot refer to it.

Be ready to be interrupted by the judge. Questions are normal and typical during closing arguments. Take it as a compliment that the judge is paying attention! Answer the judge's question as best you can and then, when the judge is finished, continue with your closing. The judge's questions may signal to you areas of weakness in your case. Be sure to address those as you continue your closing.

If the judge's questions rattle you or seem to take the other side's position, take them with a grain of salt and a polite but firm manner.

Many people make the mistake of moving away from an issue when the judge questions them on it. Don't assume that this is a weak area of your case; it could mean that the judge genuinely needs clarification or more information. If you have several more important points to make and the judge has just asked you to wrap it up, tell the judge that you have, for example, three more points to make, that you can make those points in X amount of time, and respectfully request that the Court permit you to conclude.

5. Jury Instructions

Juries need to be educated on the law. Judges will typically do this be reading out jury instructions, which explain the applicable law either at the beginning of the trial or at the end. Often, judges have already prepared jury instructions which they use for typical cases.

Sometimes, a judge will request the parties provide proposed jury instructions to him or her. The judge will use one or the other or, more likely, combine aspects of both, to read to the jury.

If you are asked to prepare proposed jury instructions, you should first see if you can obtain an example from the Court. Check with the judge's clerk or registry staff to see if they have an example. Next, you will have to research what the requirements are for you jurisdiction and type of case. Check your law library and ask the law librarian for examples.

6. Proposed Findings and Draft Proposed Order

In Chapter 6: Motions and Temporary Orders, I discussed preparing a draft order for a motion hearing. Typically, I do not offer the Court a draft order in a trial unless asked. This is because the trials I typically prepare for and have tried have been complicated and what the judge's findings (what facts the judge accepts as proven) are almost impossible to know until the close of evidence. Sometimes, at the close of evidence the judge will request "Proposed Findings of Fact and Conclusions of Law" with a draft order. When this happens, the hearing is usually postponed for a day or more so the parties can prepare their proposed findings. I do not generally recommend preparing proposed findings unless the judge requests you do so. In my experience, it would be unusual for a judge to ask a *pro se* litigant to prepare proposed findings.

So, what do you do if the judge does want proposed findings? The form of these findings will differ from jurisdiction to jurisdiction. Your first job should be to talk to the clerk's office or registry for the Court and find out what format requirements there are and to also ask if they have a sample.

Typically, these are the elements of Proposed Findings of Fact and Conclusions of Law:

1. A description of the facts told in a narrative form. In other words, tell the story of what happened. This is usually in a numbered format, like an affidavit. Everything you say has to come from the evidence at trial. Just say what you believe the evidence has proven. You should write in a neutral voice, factual voice as if the document you are writing was written by the Court. (You do not argue or say "I" in Proposed Findings.)

2. Describe the relevant law including case law and then apply the law to the facts.

3. Conclude with what should happen based on the application of law to the facts. In other words, state what you want to happen, your relief.

7. The Judge's Decision

When the judge makes his or her decision, how that decision is communicated can range from a one-liner ("The Claims of the Plaintiff are dismissed" or "The Claims of the Plaintiff are allowed") to Findings of Fact and Conclusions of Law, which details the facts that the judge has decided are proven, the law as the judge has decided it should be, and what will happen. Thus, writing Proposed Findings means you get a crack at writing what the judge might in fact use. Of course, the judge could also use the other side's proposed findings.

In a jury trial, the jury will leave the courtroom after the close of evidence and the jury instruction to take time to consider. This is known as "jury deliberations." The jury will then return and advise the judge of their decision. Juries do not give an explanation as to why they made their decision.

A judge may render his or her decision orally from the bench at the conclusion of the trial, or reserve judgement and make a written decision at a later stage. If the judge has reserved, the decision may take days or even months. If it is taking a long time, you may want to check with the judge's clerk or other registry staff to see when, if the judge has a typical time frame for issuing decisions. Also, you should check with the Court regularly in case a decision was made but not sent to you. This is important in case you want to appeal. Appeals typically must be filed very soon after the judge makes a decision; when the judge's decision is placed in the Court docket, this is known as "entry of the judgement."

Once the judge makes his or her decision, that ends the trial. If the judge makes an oral decision from the bench, you should generally not try to argue or persuade the judge to change his or her mind. However, if the judge orally makes a decision and you do not understand it, or it does not address all the claims in your case, you should politely point this out to the judge and ask for clarification.

8. Costs

Costs are how much money each side spent in preparing and going to trial. In other words, they are your legal fees, filing fees, examination fees, postage, photocopying, etc. If you win your case, in many jurisdictions you can ask the judge to order the other side to pay your costs. Often, costs are standardized and set by regulation or tariff (thus you don't get back what you actually may have paid but what the rules say you should get).

There is usually no harm in asking for costs. (Often, lawyers try to persuade the other side to accept a settlement offer by threatening that they will ask for costs when they win the case at trial.) Typically, after a judge has a made an oral decision it is an appropriate time to tell the judge that you would like to ask for costs. (This is more of a reminder because you probably asked for costs in your original Statement of Claim or Defence.) Alternatively, in some jurisdictions, if the judge's decision does not talk about whether costs are awarded, you can file a written motion asking for costs after the trial.

12

You Won (You Lost): What Next?

The judge (or jury) has made a decision, which was either:

1. From the bench. This is an oral decision. Once the judge makes an order orally, that is the law. It is effective immediately (unless the terms of the order or Court Rules specify otherwise). There will also be a written copy of the judge's order.

2. In writing. Usually, you will have received a copy in the mail. This is usually effective when it is "entered" into the case docket.

If you disagree with the Court's decision, do not delay. There is always an appeal deadline; in some cases it can be as little as one week.

1. You Won! Now What? Enforcing a Court Order

So, you won your case and there is an order that the other side pay you a certain sum of money. Congratulations! You are now a "payee," the person to whom money is supposed to be paid. You are also a "creditor." Or, maybe the order was that the other side do something such as allowing you to have increased parenting time (access) to your children.

What do you do if the other side isn't doing what the order says? For example, they were supposed to pay you a certain sum of money, but haven't. Or they are sticking to the old parenting schedule, not the one in the Court Order.

Unfortunately, this often means you may have to start another legal proceeding.

Your first step is to contact the other side and find out why they have not complied with the order. I recommend sending a polite but firm letter that requests compliance within a certain time frame and, if that time frame passes, warning them that you intend to go to court to enforce the order. In most jurisdictions, you will be able to go back to court to ask the Court to sanction (penalize) the other side if they are intentionally in violation of the Court Order. (You typically will want to wait until the appeal period has expired to do this in case they are planning on filing an appeal.)

The sanctions a court can impose are often a fine. After you check your local rules and practice, I recommend you warn the other side in your letter about any possible fines and court costs. Be careful, about any rules in your jurisdiction that prohibit harassing the person who owes you money. If you end up losing your temper or otherwise harassing the person, you could be the one in court facing a displeased judge with the power to sanction you.

In my experience, courts do not look favourably on any violation of their order when there is no good reason for noncompliance.

1.1 Going to court to enforce the order

If the other side still won't comply with the Court Order and sending a letter hasn't worked, you will probably have to start a new court proceeding to enforce the order. These are known as contempt proceedings. The following are examples of some of the tools that may be available to make the other side comply with the Court Order:

1. **Garnishee income:** Depending on your local Court Rules you may be able to ask a judge to order that the other side's employer deduct a portion of his or her paycheque to pay you.

2. **Attach a bank account:** You may be able to obtain a Court Order that requires a bank to pay to you any money in the other side's bank account. (Unfortunately, this is easy for people to get around; they will simply stop depositing money in that account.)

3. **Liens:** You may be able to place a lien (notice on title) against property such as real estate that the other side owns. Unfortunately, you will have to wait until he or she sells the property to collect your money. If, however, the other side wants to sell the property and its value is equal to or more than the lien, this can be a good way to collect your money.

These collection methods are complicated. In my experience, even lawyers struggle to make someone who doesn't want to pay actually do it. Some lawyers make their whole practice a collections practice. If the other side has no income and no assets, well, you can't get blood from a stone. See section 3.

If the other side declares bankruptcy, this generally means that you will have to stand in line with other creditors (people to whom he or she owes money) to get a portion of what is owed to you. There are rules with respect to notifying the appropriate players in the other side's bankruptcy matters. This is an issue that is beyond the scope of this book but you should do your own research right away and contact a lawyer familiar with collection and bankruptcy issues. You should not attempt further collection efforts without first familiarizing yourself with whether the other side has in fact filed for bankruptcy (instead of simply planning to) and what the rules are for you to participate in the bankruptcy matter.

I recommend you consult a lawyer for legal advice if the other side is not complying with a Court Order.

2. You Lost: Do You Have to Do What the Order Says?

If you lost, generally speaking if you do not do what a Court Order says you have to do, you may be found to have violated the order and may face penalties such as a fine. In very serious cases where a person wilfully disobeys a Court Order, he or she could face possible imprisonment. Disobeying the Court's authority by not doing what a Court Order tells you is known as being in contempt of court. If you believe you may be in contempt, you should talk to a lawyer as soon as possible.

Generally, for the other side to ask the Court to make a finding that you violated the Court Order and to order you to pay fines or other sanctions, the other side will have to file a new court action, typically called a Complaint for Contempt. Courts usually look on noncompliance unfavourably.

If the judgement is for money and you simply cannot pay the amount, one option is to request a hearing to have the order modified for a payment plan. You could also try to reach an agreement with the other side for payments (or even a lower amount) but you should enter that agreement in Court so that you are not in violation of the order. It is important to do something (i.e., go to court to explain why you cannot pay the full amount) rather than nothing as the judgement might accrue interest.

Changing a Court Order is known as "modification" or "variation." Typically, you can only modify a final Court order if there has been a material change in circumstances. This means facts have changed since the order was made.

3. Judgement Proof

Some people's income and what they own is protected by statute. Usually, these statutes are to allow people with modest resources to literally not lose everything. If all of your income and assets are protected, you are known as "judgement proof." For example, if your income is Employment Insurance money that income generally cannot be garnisheed.

Judgement proof is a misnomer because there is still a judgement saying you have to pay money; it's just that the Court is unable to make you pay that money while you are judgement proof. (The day you win the lottery or otherwise are no longer judgement proof, the other side will be able to collect from you.) There are a number of rules and types of income and assets including real estate that may mean that you are effectively judgement proof but these rules and types of income are different between jurisdictions. In British Columbia, for example, the *Court Order Enforcement Act* says that you cannot seize property jointly owned with another person (so, forget seizing a bank account the other side owns jointly with a spouse), up to $10,000 of his or her "tools of the trade," and up to $5,000 of a motor vehicle. Also, in BC, employment insurance, income assistance from the Ministry of Human Resources, or Workers' Compensation Board income cannot be garnisheed.

4. Post-Judgement Agreements

You and the other side can agree to do things differently than the Court Order specifies (e.g., if you are ordered to pay $10,000 to the Plaintiff by March 1, 20XX, but both of you agree you can pay by

March 15, 20XX). However, unless you change the Court Order, you are technically in violation of it. So, you and the other side should put your agreement in writing and ask the Court to modify the previous order. You will have to check procedures and Court Rules in your jurisdiction to do this. The risk of reaching an agreement but not asking the Court to change its order is that the other side could still take you back to court for contempt or some other person may bring this technical violation to the Court's attention. The amount owing may also be accruing interest.

5. Post-Judgement Motions

Instead of an appeal to a higher court, you may have grounds to change the Court's decision by filing a motion. You should research what options are available in your jurisdiction as these motions differ. Strict deadlines usually apply to the filing of these motions. Here are some examples of post-trial motions:

- **Motion to clarify judgement:** Sometimes the parties disagree on what the judge has actually ordered. If that happens, you may file a motion in court to ask the judge to clarify his or her decision.

- **Motion for a new trial:** A request to the Court to order a new trial because of errors made by the judge during the trial or in the judge's decision.

- **Other motions:** There may be other motions in your jurisdiction. Ones I've had reason to want to use include a motion to correct a typographic error or to correct mathematical errors. (Oops! The clerk forgot to add a couple of zeros at the end of the judgement total.)

6. Appeals

If you disagree with the Court's decision, you may be considering filing an appeal. An appeal is an application to a higher court to change a lower court's decision. (For example, in British Columbia decisions of the Supreme Court are appealed to the BC Court of Appeal.) There are strict deadlines to file an appeal.

In most jurisdictions, the person who files an appeal is the "appellant"; the person who is served with an appeal is the "respondent."

Appeals are very different from trials, and generally harder to win. There is no jury in an appeal; courts often consist of a tribunal of three or more judges. Procedures vary between jurisdictions, the type of case brought, and which court heard the case. Because of the complexity of procedure and law I do not recommend doing an appeal without the assistance of a lawyer. Appeals are expensive (e.g., there are filing fees and you have to order transcripts of what happened at trial) and hard to win.

Appeals are not usually a retrial. Instead, an appeal is an examination of what happened at trial to see if the trial judge made an error. Often the only reason you can appeal is because the judge made a significant mistake about what the law is. For example, the judge should have applied a legal rule differently, or there was a case from a higher court that the judge failed to consider. This is known as an "error of law."

What if you believe the judge's mistake was about the facts? Generally, appeals courts view the judge (or jury) as being in the very best position to make decisions about facts such as what evidence to consider and who is believable. That is because a trial judge or a jury is sitting right in the courtroom and can observe witnesses and how they react to being questioned in a way that an appeals court cannot, (i.e., only examining the written transcripts and court records). However, your jurisdiction may allow an appeal based on an error of fact.

An appeal is not usually an opportunity to present new evidence. If you do have new evidence, usually you must obtain the appeals court's permission to present it. Typically, there must be a very good reason as to why this new evidence was not available for the lower court trial.

Keep these principles in mind:

1. An appeal is usually not a new trial. An appeals court generally will not hear witnesses or conduct a rehearing of the trial. (When a court of appeal does hear the case again or sends it back to the trial court for a new trial, it is called a "hearing de novo.")

2. An appeals court will not change a lower court's decision simply because it doesn't like the decision. An appeals court can change a judge's decision if the appeals court finds that the lower court made a mistake, such as an error of law, an error of procedure or, in rare cases, an error of fact.

3. The error must generally be significant and have affected the outcome of your case. For example, spelling your witness' name wrong is not a reason for an appeal.

6.1 How appeals are made

As always, keep a careful eye on deadlines; check when an appeal must be filed and served on the other side. You should check with your court registry for the specific rules for your jurisdiction and type of case.

Typically, an appeal is begun by filing a Notice of Appeal. The notice will state your legal grounds for filing the appeal. At the same time, you may wish (or be required) to order transcripts of the trial. A Notice of Appeal must be served on the other side. If you are unsure about filing an appeal and the appeal deadline is just a day or two away, you should consider filing and serving your Notice of Appeal so that you do not lose your chance. You can usually withdraw your appeal at a later date.

In some jurisdictions, you may be required to ask for leave (or permission) to file an appeal. Such a request is generally heard in court by a judge.

Once you have filed and served the notice, there will be a deadline for you to file a statement of your reasons for the appeal. This is typically known as a "brief" or a "factum." It is the argument you will make on your hearing date to the appeal tribunal. Sometimes, appeals are decided solely on the basis of the filed brief and there is no hearing. There are usually strict rules about what must be contained in your "brief" and how long it must be, whether it has to be bound (usually spiral bound) and even, if some jurisdictions, what colour paper it can be on. You should obtain a sample copy of a brief for the same court on similar issues, if possible, before you prepare your own. For example, in British Columbia a factum to the BC Court of Appeal must not exceed 30 pages; six copies must be filed; and it must consist of a chronology of relevant dates in the litigation, an opening statement, a statement of the facts, the legal reasons for the appeal (i.e., what errors were made in the judgement), your legal argument, what you want to happen in the appeal, and a list of legal authorities (the law and cases that support your position). This is not a complete list of what you need for your brief!

6.2 What if you are served with a Notice of Appeal?

Don't panic, but prepare. Unless the trial court judge clearly messed things up, appeals are hard to win and the other side will likely have a steep uphill climb.

You should take the appeal very seriously and, the bad news is, you will have to devote your time and attention to it. Typically, you will have to file a brief or factum in response. Your job in your brief will be to explain how the lower court made the correct decision and that the appellant's grounds for appeal are wrong.

Your first priority should be to find out when your response is due.

6.3 What happens to the trial court's order while you are waiting for your appeal hearing?

While waiting on an appeal, the original trial court's decision will remain in force or it will be suspended (stayed) depending on your jurisdiction and the type of case you have. If the order remains in force, you may be able to ask the Appeals Court to suspend (stay) the lower court decision before the full appeal is heard.

So, if you are wondering what to do (do you pay the money? Do you start the kids on the new parenting schedule?), you will have to look closely at the Notice of Appeal and the Court Rules in your jurisdiction. Talking to the registry and to a lawyer is the way to go.

6.4 Is an appeal worth it? A lawyer can help

A person considering whether to file an appeal will have to decide whether it is worth the time and expense. Those served with an appeal will face a similar decision.

The issues on appeal will often be different than at trial. For this reason, a fresh legal opinion from a lawyer will be very helpful. Also, a lawyer who was unwilling to take your case to trial or perhaps had fees that were too high before may be willing to take your case for an appeal if the appeal has a good chance of winning or will make new law. Appeals that are likely to win or make new law carry a certain amount of prestige for lawyers.

6.5 The appeal hearing

An appeal hearing requires organization. If possible, watch at least one appeal hearing before your own to get a sense of how they work. Appeals Court hearings are usually more formal than Trial Court. So, dress professionally. Also, figure out how to address the judge. (For example, in British Columbia, the judges of the Court of Appeal are "my Lord" or "my Lady" or, if you want to refer to the whole panel, "the Court.")

Often you will begin to make your oral presentation and will be interrupted by a judge with a question. Prepare for these questions by trying to imagine the questions ahead of time. Think about weaknesses in your case and be prepared to address them head on.

If you are the appellant (the person bringing the appeal), you will need to have detailed notes on why you feel the judge erred, the places in the transcript or judge's written decision that indicate error, and the legal basis (statutes and case law) that support your argument.

If you are the respondent, you will want to explain that the judge made the correct decision. You will want to attack the appellant's grounds for appeal.

If possible, arrange to meet with a lawyer for coaching on how to present your argument beforehand.

7. Modifications: Changing the Court's Order in the Future

What happens if the Court Order that was made is now inappropriate because of a change in circumstances? For example, if a Court Order set a parenting schedule for a child who was three years old but now is school age, can the order be changed? Typically, you can apply to change a Court Order if there has been a significant change in the circumstances since the order was made. How significant that change has to be will depend on the law in your jurisdiction.

Modifications are generally new applications. That means, you will have to file and serve a new application or complaint.

8. When Is It Over?

Once the gates of litigation have been opened, it is hard to close them. Generally, in most civil proceedings once judgement has been entered, the appeal period has expired, and whatever was ordered to be done is done (e.g., payment in full is made), the case is over. There are exceptions, but they are rare (e.g., if significant new evidence is discovered, it may be possible to reopen a case).

Some types of proceedings do not wind down easily. For example, family law proceedings can lead to modification applications as long as there are dependent children or some form of support is being paid. That is another reason why less costly forms of dispute resolution — such as mediation where the parties use a trained professional to work out solutions for themselves — are a good idea.

9. What Do You Do with All the Stuff?

You will have accumulated binders, evidence, and notes, not to mention correspondence, unused office supplies, and perhaps an increased coffee consumption habit. Until the appeal period expires, you should keep all the binders, evidence, and notes. If there is an appeal, you may need to reuse some of this material. If there is no appeal, this is what I keep:

1. **All pleadings and exhibits:** In other words, everything filed in court. These could become important if a party later needs to enforce a Court Order or if a party wants to try to change it (a modification).

2. **Correspondence and notes:** For a lawyer, there's a duty here, but for the non-lawyer, I also recommend keeping letters. This is because those letters provide a glimpse into what was happening outside of the courtroom. Were there settlement discussions? How were the parties and lawyers behaving? If there are further legal proceedings (e.g., to enforce the Court Order or to change it), there might be useful information in these papers.

3. **Discovery:** I recommend keeping the information disclosed to you and your original copies of your exhibits for at least a year in case of a late-filed appeal, modification, or with respect to an action to enforce the Court Order.

Your Trial Book, any extra copies of things, and case law, you can discard. Because these documents likely contain confidential information, I recommend shredding and securely disposing them.

10. Congratulations

Going to court, for an unrepresented person, can feel like going to war and learning a new language at the same time. At the end of the day, whether you win or lose, mounting a trial is a mammoth undertaking and you are no doubt exhausted. You probably have a scar or two! A trial usually can be counted on for at least one thing: An end to the uncertainty. You have your decision.

Regardless of whether you won or lost, you should be proud of standing up for yourself. In an ideal world, a lawyer probably should have been there for you; our legal aid system and high legal fees leave so many with no choice but to go to court unrepresented, and the system was not designed for unrepresented people.

Facing so much uncertainty and strangeness, you weren't defeated by the court system. Whether you won or lost, I want to congratulate you on running the race. You did it!

Download Kit

Please enter the URL you see in the box below into your computer web browser to access and download the kit.

> **www.self-counsel.com/updates/represent_can/15kit.htm**

The download kit includes:

- Sample clauses for settlement agreements and consent orders
- Tips for avoiding affidavit wars
- Glossary of legal terms
- — And more!